TO HELL AND BACK

TO HELL AND BACK

How I Survived
Wall Street's Roller Coaster
...and How You Can Too!

KEN STERN

Dearborn™
Trade Publishing
A **Kaplan Professional** Company

Vice President and Publisher: Cynthia A. Zigmund
Editorial Director: Donald J. Hull
Senior Project Editor: Trey Thoelcke
Interior Design: Lucy Jenkins
Cover Design: Design Alliance, Inc.
Typesetting: the dotted i

Library of Congress Cataloging-in-Publication Data

Stern, Ken, 1965–
    To hell and back : how I survived Wall Street's roller coaster and how you can too / Ken Stern.
      p.   cm.
    ISBN 0-7931-4922-3 (6x9 hdbk)
    1. Investments—United States. 2. Stocks—United States. 3. Investment analysis. 4. Wall Street. I. Title.
HG4910 .S663 2002
332.63′22—dc21

2001004680

CONTENTS

ACKNOWLEDGMENTS

This book was made possible through the hard work of many individuals. I want to thank everyone at Asset Planning Solutions, Inc., and Ken Stern & Associates. Their dedication to our cause is a strong motivator.

In writing this book we found that Luanne's skills extend beyond compliance. Her suggestions, editing, and ideas were right on.

Cynthia Zigmund, Dearborn vice president, and everyone else at Dearborn—you guys are great. Most of all, I thank my family for putting up with me and for teaching me the definition of unconditional love. Rachael Marie, you make me want to be better. Never forget, you can do anything you want to do. I love you.

INTRODUCTION

"The harder you fall, the higher you bounce." —Anonymous

Look around and tell me what you see. I see people scrambling to stay ahead of the curve.

Forget simply staying ahead of the curve. *To Hell and Back* is designed to provide you with a strategy, a process to get way ahead of the curve. A process to thrive during all kinds of environments, including times of economic uncertainty and shaky stock markets.

It is time to start or strengthen your business, to make savvy investments, to find hidden wealth, and to get ahead—way ahead.

It has been said that all men are created equal. OK, fine. But I want, and I assume you also want, to be more than equal. I want to make fewer mistakes, to be better. I want to master life. There is no doubt, regardless of who you are or your station in life, that you can master life.

Of course, it is possible to master life with limited wealth. Personally, I prefer unlimited wealth. I prefer mastering the challenge of creating wealth and enjoying myself during this lifelong process.

At first blush it appears truly amazing that wealth evades most who seek it. It is even more amazing when you look at the number of people who had wealth and lost it, and it's sad to see all the others who are successful at building wealth but still are unhappy.

The first reason wealth and happiness elude so many people is poor preparation. The second is failure to seek an adequate base of specific knowledge, and the third is not being disciplined.

If you are truly ready to learn, then you have chosen the right book. But you need more than a desire. You must be willing to work at it. The magic elixir I am offering is not a get-rich-quick scheme. Within these pages I offer an instructional manual for the accumulation of wealth and the pursuit of happiness—all the tools you need are here. The only missing ingredient is you!

If you are willing to use this book as it is intended, if you are willing to make a commitment to focusing on the process, then your actions should manifest that commitment.

This book is divided into five separate parts. Read them all, preferably in the order presented. I have read many excellent financial planning books on subjects ranging from stock picking to economics, from financial planning to budgeting. As a result, I have found that if you devote all your attention to the singular ingredient you feel is the most important, success will elude you. For instance, at this point you may not see the wisdom in learning about the importance of the Federal Reserve. But you soon will. You must have all the ingredients to understand the process. You must have a process to reach the pinnacle of success.

MY OWN STORY

Throughout my life I have made many mistakes, some dumb, others not so dumb. Through these mistakes I have formed a process. Provided I follow this process, I will be successful. I went to Hell, and now I am back. Take this knowledge I'm going to share with you, add it to your own unique knowledge base, and you should find success as well.

Take comfort in the knowledge that there is a happy ending. As the title of this book indicates, I went to Hell (my personal, and probably my family's, Hell), and I not only survived but I thrived! In fact, I am a more prosperous, happier, and better person than ever. I hope you more than enjoy this story—I hope you hug the bear and take the bull by the horns. It is my sincere hope you will use the knowledge offered here to make money in any market at any time.

It was March 10, 2000. I was on top of the world! Life was awesome! Business was great! My family had just bought a big new house. My investments were going to the moon. On top of it all, it was my birthday. The only problem was a little voice (the voice of reason) that kept whispering in my conscious thoughts. When you invest other people's hard-earned money, as I do, being cautious and skeptical is not only healthy; it's what you get paid to do. But this little voice was such a party pooper; I tried to push it back into my subconscious as much as possible.

Ironically, I had gone on record a year earlier, 1999, in a speech about the idiotic investor. I talked about ridiculous valuations of technology stocks. I talked about the importance of value and the differences between buying companies and stocks. I sold some Cisco & Yahoo! (just not enough). Because of this conservative approach, my performance (track record as a money manager), while OK, was not great in 1999. Hard to believe, but I invested in (gasp!) boring stocks, not the hot dot-coms of the day: food stocks, some retail stocks, and other stocks traditionally considered defensive plays. I thought these investments were good deals. They were being ignored because the only investments that saw any buying activity were technology based. Worse, my investments weren't moving, meaning they weren't making money for me (or my clients). Quite frankly, I began to question my investment style. It was lonely out there all by myself. My clients questioned my investment style. They wanted higher and higher returns, regardless of the risk.

I talked to other investment managers, who would expound the virtues of "the new market." How the new paradigm had changed investment rules. It begins to weigh on your psyche when your cab drivers are on their cell phones day trading stocks—for big profits. My employees bought me stuffed bears and laughed. They laughed because they were doubling and tripling their investments in their own trading accounts—the ones *I* didn't manage. *Even my best friend decided not to invest with me because he was doing better on his own!*

So I altered my investment style. I didn't stick to my discipline. I increased my exposure to growth sectors. Of course, I was most aggressive with my own funds. Stupid, stupid, stupid!

Soon after my birthday, all hell broke loose. The markets began dropping. The mantra was "a great buying opportunity." Then more money was lost. Pretty soon there would be no extra money to take advantage of these so-called buying opportunities. I wasn't so sure it was, in fact, a great buying opportunity.

One year later, on March 10, 2000, the Nasdaq had shed more than 60 percent of its value. Having retreated roughly 20 percent, Standard & Poor's 500-stock index was officially in bear market territory.

The first time I began to second-guess myself, I didn't lose money. That was in 1999, when I was buying defensive stocks and not making very much money. Not making much money is far better then losing money. But it is when you start buying growth stocks right before a bear market that you do much worse than not making much money: you lose money—and lose money I did.

I am paid to figure out ways to make money for people. My belief was to buy great companies: the price would eventually be recognized in the stock sooner or later. I still hold to that belief. But when a strategy doesn't work for a reasonable period of time, it's human nature to rethink one's strategy. Common phrases I heard at the time included, "Why fight the tape?"; "The trend is your friend"; "Do what works"; and my favorite: "You are a dinosaur, Ken!"

As the markets dropped and dropped, a dark shadow came over me. Will I feed my family? Lose the house or business? My wife is thinking that we can't go on vacation, and I'm thinking about losing the house!

I became irritable, repressed, and went into my cave. I was losing money; the markets continued to drop. At this stage, it's very easy to become myopic, to see only the negative. As a result, I was lashing out, losing sleep, and wondering what happened to my great life. My family was upset with me, and so were my coworkers. It was a terrible time! Then something wonderful happened. After a particularly bad day, I had a meeting with myself. I took inventory. I asked myself what my strengths and weaknesses were. I found out what was important to me. Was I the best person to manage money for my clients and myself? Thankfully, I answered, *"Yes!"* I was the best person to manage the money. Needless to say, it didn't take long for me to get back. I survived and thrived during the worst bear market in the history of the over-the-counter market.

I went back to the fundamentals (literally). I believed in my investment strategy again. I went back to the strategy that had brought me where I am today but had unwisely begun to abandon in 1999. I found my second wind and became very excited going to work each day. I even got excited when the markets dropped. Even more important, I was excited spending time with my family and even excited on the days my portfolio went down (this was and is a clever feat you will learn in upcoming pages).

THE DIFFERENCE BETWEEN GOOD AND GREAT

Great investors practice, are curious, stay focused, and act on their convictions. Great investors also make mistakes, go through bad cycles, and sometimes want to quit. The truly great investors don't quit. They persist and persevere.

It is not just your analytical ability and not just your ability to spot a market trend that will make you a world-class investor. It is bringing the entire process together that makes the difference.

By the way, will I make mistakes in the future? You bet. And so will you. Admit it. We are the same; you are a recovering perfectionist, too. Remember to learn from your mistakes instead of creating (or feeding) an ulcer. Relish and enjoy the learning experience. You and I will get better from every experience, every time.

I write this a little over one year later. Ironically, I'm smarter and have increased my investments. So I'm taking a break, sitting here smoking a cigar. Cigars are a waste of money to some (I think this little number cost $10) but I have a philosophy: everyone should have one vice (not two). When you hit a goal, reward yourself. I met the goals I set for myself today. I deserve the cigar! I'm back from Hell and ready to rock! Please don't think I will never have bad days, or down days in the market. Both will happen. One only needs to look to the unexpected, devastating, and horrific terrorist events that collapsed the World Trade Center, and Wall Street's subsequent sell off for proof. However, no matter what, I will not allow emotions to dictate my investment policy.

Before I propose my thoughts and findings about what's necessary to thrive in any market, any time, you must agree (it's OK, actually beneficial, to be a bit skeptical) with the following. If you can't agree and embrace the following six truisms, this book will waste your time:

1. Investing is both a science and an art. You are capable of being a successful investor.
2. If you stick to your discipline and your plan, the rest is easy.
3. Acquiring wealth and being a good investor is as much a lifestyle as it is being a good stock picker.
4. Attitude is essential.
5. Consciously or unconsciously, you have an arsenal of skills that will help you achieve your goals.
6. It is possible to make money during any market environment.

HOW TO USE THIS BOOK

You will be exposed to many different strategies in this book. Some you will utilize, others you won't. Some of the strategies are incredibly easy to implement and may seem to contradict another strategy. There is more than one way to skin a cat.

In fact, there may be an overabundance of information burdening you with information overload. The best advice I can give you is to read this book *in its entirety,* pick the strategy or strategies you feel work best for you, and then stick to them. Having discipline, a strategy, and knowledge is more important than being a good market forecaster or stock picker.

Throughout the book you will see various rules that I formed during my journey to Hell and back, and from these rules a school was erected. It's called Ken Stern's School of Common Sense. The rules function as guides to the treasure map. Pick them up along the way and make them your rules. Undoubtedly, they'll save you time, money, and probably lots of aggravation. Best of all, they should help you make some extra dough.

Prepare

PART ONE

CHAPTER ONE

Ken Stern's
School of Common Sense

THE SKY IS FALLING

Wouldn't you love it if I had a crystal ball that could tell you everything you wanted to know? Well, lucky for you, I do, although you may not like the information I have.

Let me give it to you straight: we are going to have a recession. We are going to have hyperinflation. Our president is going to get shot. We are going to be at war and face the threat of nuclear annihilation. The United States will come under siege from terrorist attacks that will rock Wall Street and cause the deaths of thousands of people. As I said, it doesn't sound too good, does it?

You may have surmised that all of this has happened over the past several years. My crystal ball looks into the past.

In the last 70 years we have had several doom-and-gloom periods. Actually, that's stating the situation mildly. Figure 1.1 is a chart that you have probably seen if you have dabbled at investing. It follows Standard & Poor's 500-stock index, beginning in 1920 and ending at the end of the first quarter of 2001.

Look at some of the entries. I included the most traumatic and trying economic situations that occurred during that period:

Look carefully at Figure 1.1. As bad as things became at times and as bad as things may someday become, you could have profited from these occurrences had you been ready. There is much wealth to be made. There are many ways to prepare and plan for seemingly surprise

FIGURE 1.1   S&P versus Inflation

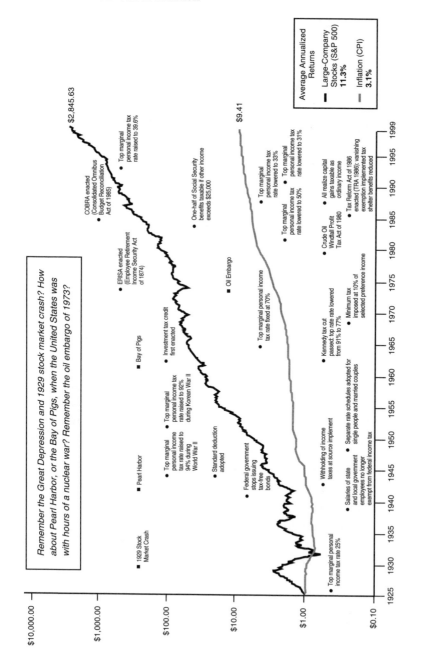

FIGURE 1.2   DJIA Declines and Their Frequency

Dow Jones Industrial Average Declines	Average Frequency of Declines
5% or more	About 3.5 times per year
10% or more	About once per year
15% or more	About 1 every 2 years
20%	About 1 every 3 years

---

events. It's no surprise to see, after the fact, how obvious a seeming surprise should have been. Now if you don't follow a formula and don't garner the necessary knowledge, you're going to be a sitting duck all over again. Surprise! Your success will be limited to say the least.

Don't think I'm making light of a serious subject: bear markets are serious. Positioned properly, they are also a serious way to make money. They are also not that uncommon, as shown in Figure 1.2.

THE FORMULA

Use the flowchart in Figure 1.3 as your guide. Before skipping to the investment chapters, create your personal wealth plan (PWP), a subject that is a book in and of itself. Although I have very strong views on the subject, many incredible books on financial planning and time management already exist, so my book outlines what I believe to be the critical broad strokes. Once you have created your PWP and know what you are trying to accomplish financially, you will learn how to strategize and invest during different market cycles. This sounds easy enough, but, believe me, without discipline, trusting your instincts is next to impossible. Sticking to your discipline is going to take a great deal of mental training, so don't take this step lightly.

Some of you may be saying, "Fine. Get on with it. Show me how to find which stocks are going to double." Even if I show you, you can still lose—I did! Some incredibly talented investors fail every day. The differentiating factors are *discipline, farsightedness,* and *correct attitude.* The only reasons I was able to get back from Hell so fast and thrive during the last bear market: I never forgot what put me on top in the first place; knowing my strengths; and relying on a solid wealth plan that had been created years before. It's true that I lost my discipline and almost sold my soul, but ultimately I kept the faith. There's no shortcut, folks.

FIGURE 1.3   The Successful Investor

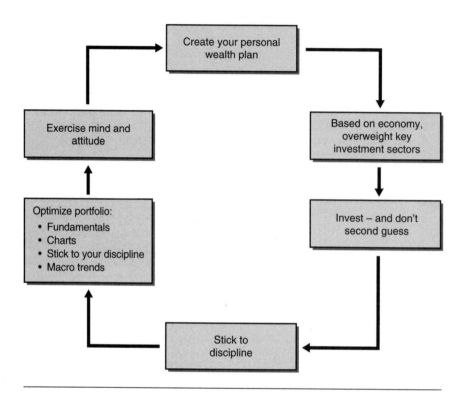

The flowchart in Figure 1.3 is a recipe. Follow it closely until you get the hang of it. If you follow the recipe, voila! You get a gourmet's life!

First, learn the basics. Find a good book of basic investing definitions. One of my favorites is *Barron's Dictionary of Finance and Investment Terms.* Second, read this book *in its entirety.* I've said this already, but it's worth repeating. Every subject is interrelated. Although it's important to know how to analyze the business cycle, knowledge of fundamental stock criteria is critical as well. So like a good chef, read the entire recipe before you begin the process. *To Hell and Back* covers many financial terms, but many of the strategies are more advanced. A solid grasp of the basics is in order.

DON'T FORGET TO LOOK ON THE BRIGHT SIDE AND KEEP A SENSE OF HUMOR

As bad as it gets, remember what's important. Never forget that everything is cyclical; with the right attitude, education, and discipline, you will survive and thrive from the experience too. But if that fails, look at the situation like this:

- Your repairmen, handyman, and gardener might even return your call.
- Super Bowl commercials will get back to beer and away from dot-coms.
- The time saved not watching your portfolio or day trading could be spent with your family (or fishing).
- The prospect of retirement scared you anyway.
- Mr. Jones will finally stop bragging about how much he made from Yahoo! and will stop saying "I told you so."
- You can return to Vegas for your gambling pleasure—at least in Vegas you get a free drink when you lose money.
- You can start making Yuppie jokes again.

SUMMARY: A WORD ABOUT THE VALIDITY OF THE INFORMATION

It's always great fun to speak to a bunch of academic scholars who spend countless hours proving formulas to outsmart the market. They spend their time creating scales that will tell you for certain how to value a company, or how to determine what stage of the business cycle we are in, or when to move money from cash to stocks.

Although I would never knock academia, remember that scholars are guessing too. Valuing a company requires making an educated guess. While a few formulas will be presented throughout these pages, it is not this book's focus. In fact, many of these complicated formulas don't mean a hill of beans in practice. Most of the ideas and strategies in this book are user-friendly for the layperson.

I'll show you the theories that work for me: use them to your advantage. Develop others if you like. *But stay educated, disciplined, focused, and enjoy the journey.*

CHAPTER TWO

Investing Is a Lifestyle

"If you weather the storm, you will reach the port."
—Unknown

Over the years you have heard amazing stories of incredible savers who create wealth. Recently, I was listening to Paul Harvey on the radio. He spoke of a couple that would scour Los Angeles for ten hours every night in an effort to find and collect bottles for recycling. This job and a shrewd savings plan paid for their home and put two children through college. As the story goes, their kids were graduating college with advanced degrees. In addition, this couple had saved enough money to comfortably retire.

You also hear stories of a person providing a few dollars to a friend to start a company (seed capital) those few dollars turning into millions. Other people create wealth by winning the lottery. And believe it or not, some people make millions by investing in the stock market.

Great, but here is the problem: Do you really want to be a bottle gatherer? Not me! I don't want to be on a budget *that* tight nor do I want to scour anything. If you can't enjoy the journey, why bother?

RULE If you don't love it, don't do it!

In the case of providing seed money, let's just agree that if someone asks you to invest in a "great deal," there's probably a catch. It could be that more than a few smart people passed on it before it landed in your lap. Unless you truly understand the business, the management, and the deal, I caution you against start-ups. For every person you hear that struck it rich, hundreds of others lose their investment.

RULE Investors make money on deals they pass up.

I remember when the market was going gangbusters. All the people I knew who worked for publicly traded companies thought they had a surefire investment strategy: Accumulate all the company stock options available to them for about five years, cash in for a couple of million, and enjoy the rest of their life.

People that worked for great companies like Qualcomm, Microsoft, Motorola, and Cisco thought this way. This strategy may prove successful in the long term, at least while I am writing this, but the plan didn't pan out too well. Worse, a lot of those people are looking for jobs.

RULE Always have a plan B.

Many of those same people who trade in their Mercedes every few years have less than six months of expenses in cash reserves, and now they are worried about being laid off! Don't join that group. Always have a plan B.

MONEY

How do you feel about money? Do you respect it? Truly respect it? Do you treat it well? If you honestly do, it will treat you well. If not, it's going to be much harder to grasp the concepts laid out here.

Luckily, I do appreciate money. The more money I make, the more I respect money. Driving a nice car provides me little pleasure. So to shell out lots of money for transportation irks me terribly. I would rather spend the money on a landscaper, so that I can spend the extra time with my family. As a result, I find better values when buying automobiles and use the savings to do what is important to me.

The way I look at it: everything—and I mean *everything*—in your life can be viewed as an investment. To me, a car is a bad investment, so I try to minimize the loss. Using a credit card is an investment. If the money I could borrow from a credit card would make more money for me somewhere else, then I wouldn't mind using the credit card. Unfortunately, the cost of the credit card usually nullifies any investment returns I could comfortably make. Besides, most people use credit cards for expenses, not investments. I keep debt on my house because the money it would take to pay off my mortgage actually makes more money in other investments. I see my mortgage as positive debt, at least right now. The debt is cheap; I invest the difference and get a tax write-off for keeping it. It's a good investment.

I'll even invest in a vacation; that's an investment in myself. Everything in your life can be viewed as an investment. The $5 a day you spend at the vending machine can be viewed as an investment. If you spend $25 a week ($100 a month) in the vending machines, that one "investment" can really add up—most likely not in your bank account but around your waistline! If, 20 years ago, you put the same money in the stock of a leading growth company, that investment could be worth hundreds of thousands of dollars today.

RULE Respect money, and begin to see your lifestyle as an investment.

Instead of picking up recyclable bottles or worrying about stock options, try Ken Stern's Commonsense Rules for accumulating wealth.

KEN STERN'S COMMONSENSE RULES FOR ACCUMULATING WEALTH

RULE Be clever about finding extra income.

RULE Have an autopilot investing strategy.

RULE Keep a reserve.

RULE Treat everything like a business.

RULE Invest only in what you know and understand.

Be Clever about Finding Extra Income

If you are self-employed, save money in such tax-saving vehicles as IRAs, SEP-IRAs, and KEOGH plans. Not only do you force yourself to save, but you get a tax deduction as well.

You can also be clever with small amounts of wasted cash ($5 per day at lunch, $7 car washes, etc.). I know it seems trivial, but *small amounts of money add up to large amounts of money.*

Have an Autopilot Investment Strategy

Autopilot investing is the art of paying yourself first. Religiously, without thought or choice, 10 percent of your gross income should be withdrawn from your paycheck or bank account every pay period. It should be deposited in a direct stock plan, a great mutual fund, or a brokerage account. Regardless of market conditions, this percent of your gross income is never touched—ever! At least, not until your goal is achieved (let's assume that goal is retirement).

Assume you gross $70,000 per year. That means you will be investing about the same amount you spend on a few car payments. You need the savings more than the nice car. Over the past 20 years, a $7,000-a-year investment could have grown to $500,000 in a top-performing mutual fund. (I assumed that the account would earn what the market or one of the top-performing mutual funds has earned over the last 20 years. Obviously, no guarantees exist that past returns could be duplicated. But if they could, or if the returns were better, think about it. One-half of a million dollars for staying disciplined?)

If you're going to engage autopilot investing, read the chapter on model portfolios and autopilot investing. Make certain you diversify your funds. Please don't put the funds in your company's stock.

Keep a Reserve

You need six months of expenses in your bank or money market account. Divide whatever you spend over the course of an entire year by two and stick it in your account. If you don't have it, build it.

You are forbidden to invest until it's there. In fact, it wouldn't hurt to have more than that in reserve; that way, you'll have that little extra to invest at the right time if an outstanding investment opportunity comes along (like a recession).

Treat Everything Like a Business

Your personal affairs should be viewed as a business. You, like all businesses, have a goal of accumulating and appreciating assets. Your home and your car are tangible investments; one appreciates, but the other doesn't.

You could even argue that clothes are an investment. If you have ever heard me speak or seen me on TV, I hope you noticed my taste in clothes—I like them! My suits are all designer-labelled and custom-tailored. I don't spend a great deal of time looking for a deal, nor do I spend a great deal of money on a suit, but I save time *and* money. How?

I get on sample-sale lists and wait for an "invite" to one of the sales. I plan my purchases around these sales and avoid impulse buying. If I need an article of clothing before the sale, you will find me at The Men's Wearhouse, which has "good" prices. Guess what? I owned the stock too. I took whatever I saved on the suits to buy more of the stock. It's a simple but effective system.

Invest Only in What You Know and Understand

I am sure somebody could make money from shrimp farms in Mexico. But I don't know the Mexican laws, how to raise shrimp, or if I can trust those operating the businesses. So I don't invest in Mexican shrimp farms. Period.

For the same reason, I try to avoid investing in brand-new, small, start-up companies. Even if there's an apparent chance for making "big money"—if the deal works—I won't invest in what I don't know and understand. If I understand the business, know the management, and believe in the project, I gladly consider investing. So I stick to what I know and let investments I don't understand go to those who may understand them better.

OK, KEN, BUT WHAT ABOUT INVESTING IN STOCKS?

I don't want to oversimplify the magnitude, complexity, or difficulty of becoming a world-class investor. I believe it requires many factors, including good timing, knowledge of the industry in which you are investing, a sufficient understanding of the economy and stock market

> **GARP.** *Growth at reasonable prices*

cycles, and a solid grasp of valuation methods. The more you have to invest, the more you will understand and respect money and the better investor you will be.

Investing is a lifestyle. It's not simply picking good stocks.

Many people talk about different styles of investing. I have heard people state they make money as a buy-and-hold investor, a value investor, a momentum investor, a technician, or a GARP investor, and so on. Although various strategies might produce the same desired outcome, living through Hell reaffirmed my belief in sticking to my discipline. The more you can accomplish this, the more your investment results will rely on science and skill and less on luck. If you are not willing to commit to a disciplined approach, you may as well head over to the casino. At least there you are guaranteed a free drink!

My sandbox, whose major features are shown in Figure 2.1, looks like this:

- Determine where we are in the economic cycle.
- Use this information to decide which sector to invest in.
- Using fundamental as well as technical data, find the best stocks in that sector and overweight that sector.

FIGURE 2.1   Stock-Picking Advice for Investors

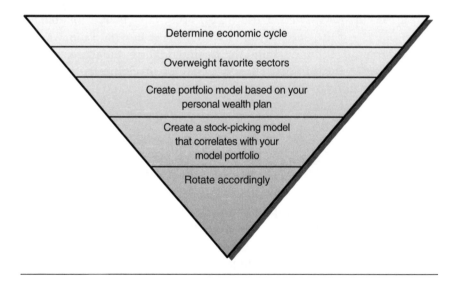

- Determine when to rotate that sector, which requires a sell discipline for your current holdings.
- Never, ever invest in something you don't understand.

DOESN'T BUY AND HOLD WORK BEST?

It sounds so easy. Buy a stock and forget about it. Over time, cyclic swings will even out and the investment should bring a better result than an active timing approach will.

This rationale is not flawed. Most people who do buy and hold outperform those who are constantly chasing the market. However, which stocks or sectors do you buy and hold? And if you can identify opportunities based on the business cycle and opportunities in the market created by it, why not capitalize on them? Many asset allocation studies have proven that moving assets between various investment classes at the right time will lead to higher returns.

I agree with the notion that timing the market is dangerous. Taking money out of the market could mean you will miss the next boom cycle, the markets move fast. Study after study has shown that even if you had invested on the day the market was at its highest point each year, investors could still have beaten other investment classes, such as cash. (See Figure 2.2.)

The investment strategies presented here are not meant to time the market. They are meant to add a turboboost to a long-term strategy.

Just to bring the point home: As of April 1, 2001, had you owned Motorola during the past five years, you would be basically flat. However, during that period, there were many negative signs that, if heeded and the stock sold because of these signs, would have allowed you to reap a profit.

Take the example of two Dow stocks, Caterpillar (CAT) and General Electric (GE). Had you invested $10,000 in either of these stocks 67 years ago, the $10,000 in GE would have grown to about $7 million, but CAT would have been a different story. First, CAT was added to the Dow in 1991, replacing Navistar. So assume you had previously bought Navistar, sold it because it was moving out of the Dow, then invested the proceeds in CAT. Your $10,000 would have been worth only about $20,000 at the end of 2000. Both investments made money, but one made a lot more. My argument is not that you should invest in only one stock and let it ride. In fact, this book is designed to teach the antithesis of that strategy. Your chance of selecting only one stock that turns out to be the best performer over 50 years is

FIGURE 2.2   The Misleading Piggy Bank Hypothesis

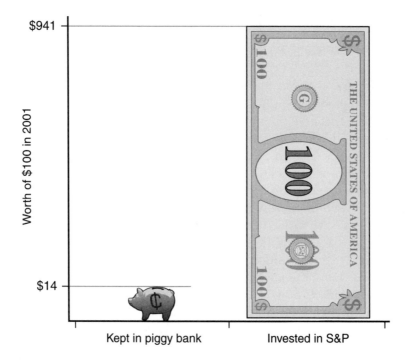

The misleading piggy bank hypothesis: An analysis of the average real return of $100 invested in the S&P 500 versus a $100 put in the piggy bank (adjusted for inflation) – from 1950 to the present.

almost zero. Investing a properly managed portfolio can lead to both superior returns and reduced risk.

CURIOSITY MAY HAVE KILLED THE CAT, BUT . . .

. . . it brought me back from Hell and makes an investor very successful. Curiosity is a trademark of successful investors. I often can learn more at a bar than I can in an analyst's meeting.

An example: A few months ago, while talking with a friend who sold a certain type of high-tech equipment, I asked if all his sales had died during the terrible bear market. He conceded that sales had dropped precipitously on all counts. When I then asked if any one company was outselling another, he told me that one of the smaller companies he represented was gaining market share, as it was selling a similar piece of equipment at a lower price than the competition. The type of equipment it sold was still necessary during the slowdown, but purchasing companies had become more cost conscious. I stated that the product might be inferior and that, after the slowdown, the bigger companies would probably take back most of the market share. He replied that the case was exactly the opposite; everyone loved the smaller company's product, and it was performing wonderfully. He said purchasing companies simply had not been inclined to try a new product during the expansion when cost controls were not an important issue. The market downturn had given this company the opportunity it needed.

After our conversation, I tracked the stock and found that sales did look as though they were holding up, but the stock dropped far more than the stock of a larger competitor. Thus, an anomaly surfaced because of my curiosity.

I rely on my curiosity when I talk to my daughter's friends about clothing trends or when I talk to my friend Jim, a truck driver hauling product around. Who is he hauling stuff for? What's the buzz? Who isn't shipping as much? Who is gaining market share? Be curious!

SUMMARY

It sure is fun talking with my friends about various stocks. I get some great research ideas that way. It's even more fun to pull the trigger and actually buy a stock. Unfortunately, it's only fun, not a serious investment—unless I do the research and decide if the stock fits into my discipline. In fact, buying a stock on a whim is gambling. I remember reading something that Donald Trump once said when asked if he gambled much. He stated that he liked the odds better being a casino owner.

I have been to Hell, briefly. It wasn't very much fun. I knew how to get out, and this time I'll stay out, permanently.

Understanding and respecting money and following my discipline will keep me on top. Casino owners play the odds and win; gamblers do the opposite. It's all a matter of deciding which side of the table you want to sit on.

CHAPTER THREE

Shields, Swords, and Strikes: Forming Your Personal Wealth Plan

In Hell, because things become distorted, I second-guessed myself. I was ready, along with everyone else, to throw in the towel; to break out, I treated the situation like the war it was. I gathered strength and confidence in the simple exercise of identifying what I was dealing with: where I had protection (shields), where I was strong (swords), and what my negatives were (strikes). Although I didn't know it at the time, this was the process of forming a personal wealth plan.

In a way this concept is similar to the one Sun Tzu states in the famous book *Art of War.* He states that most battles are won before they are ever fought. How true this is! The army with the better plan that is better prepared, excited, and knows how to act in many different conditions will win. Further, we should realize that war is inevitable, so always prepare.

The reason I lost a few battles was because I got lazy and greedy. The reason I was able to pull out so fast was because I was better prepared. I didn't have any excess debt, I had knowledge on my side, and I could pounce on the right situation. I knew my *shields, swords, and strengths.*

For a minute, forget the accounting aspects of the balance sheet you just created and think about its practical aspects. Ask yourself these questions:

- What are your strengths and weaknesses (shields and swords)?
- Are you positioned correctly with most of your assets in the big jar?

- Which expenses are you absolutely sure can be minimized?
- Which do you think could be minimized, but you are not sure how?

SHIELDS

Cash in the Bank

When taking inventory, it is a good idea to remember that cash is king. Cash allows you more leverage at work should you wish to make a job move. It could provide available funds for future investments. A good rule of thumb is to have six months of expenses in immediately accessible accounts.

Knowledge

If you are an expert in a certain field or have certain traits that make you professionally marketable, you have a definite shield during an economic downturn. You can use your expertise to make investments in the area in which you are knowledgeable. Your expertise should also make your job more secure.

Cost of a Vice. Not to pick on smokers (remember my cigars?), but have you ever calculated what smoking costs you? In California, cigarettes cost about $4.50 a pack. For a pack-a-day smoker, that comes to $135 a month or roughly $1,650 a year! With compounding interest, you could turn those funds into a small fortune rather than watch them go up in smoke!

Zero Debt

Debt can make you or break you. To have zero debt is a definite shield; it means that you have more access to capital if things get bad for a while. It means that your expenses can be minimized, as you don't have a large debt to service.

Minimizing Large Purchases for Anything That Does Not Appreciate

I understand washers and dryers do not appreciate, but we need to own them. But I don't need fancy cars, the most fashionable furniture, or similar luxuries. Choose one vice, enjoy it, and stick with it.

What is a vice? Buying lunch everyday. Smoking. Beer. You may call these items luxuries, but too many luxuries become vices because they limit your resources. Luxuries become habits and are hard to live without. However, take any one of these luxuries and figure out what it costs you. The cost could be a determining factor in the amount of wealth you can accumulate.

SWORDS

Many aspects of your plan can be used as offensive items.

Credit, Bank Lines, or Margin Interest

These are methods to access capital, but some people don't have access to capital when times get tough. Having good credit can give you a head start when times get bad.

Margin interest is tricky and should only be used very, very sparingly. Most brokerage firms will lend investors money against the investments they own; and investors use the money to purchase more investments. When all the relevant factors make sense, buying securities on margin can be an aggressive, offensive way to capitalize on an investment you view as a good opportunity.

> **M**argin. *Credit extended by brokerage companies. The amount of credit extended is based on the holdings in the account. Margin can be used to buy more shares of stock, but you do pay interest on margin.*

Never underestimate the risk of margin. Margin is a loan, a debt, so it must be repaid. If the stocks that you purchase on margin drop in value, you will have to come up with more money to satisfy the brokerage firm's margin requirement. If you don't have the money, the brokerage firm has the right to sell the stocks you own—at any price—to pay off your debt. Many people have used margin too aggressively and have lost vast sums of money in the process. Be sure to understand margin and how to use it before deciding to gamble with it. Be sure you know each brokerage firm's rules for margin and keeping a margin balance.

General Knowledge

Although they are not on the balance sheet, you have other swords—knowledge for example. You are, in some form or another, part of the economic process. The services you use and products you consume are part of the economic food chain. You know which products are better than others. You know which services are better values. At work, you know which suppliers are better and which companies you need to do business with. This knowledge is critical when investing.

Through work you may see some vendors or suppliers perform exceptionally well, excellent information to assist you in making investments. Stay curious and observant. Even writing down interesting developments or bits of information on a ledger may be useful.

Of course, lack of knowledge can be a strike as well.

When I was in Hell, I began paying attention to details again. In the Stern household, my wife and I share responsibilities. One of her responsibilities is to pay the monthly bills and keep the budget that we devised. We used to watch our budget very closely and even had a monthly budget meeting. During the good old days, we stopped having this meeting; and frankly, I didn't even look at our checking account statements.

As a fluke one day, I opened up our checking account statement and was shocked at the balance. I immediately called a family budget meeting (my wife and I in attendance). We reviewed the monthly bills and calculated how much we were spending over budget and where. My wife argued that the expenses were necessary. After reviewing every check, every charge, and even where we spent every ATM withdrawal, we both agreed that many items were not necessary. We didn't need to spend $1,000 a month for food. We didn't need to spend the kind of money we were on travel and entertainment. My daughter didn't need a new toy every time we went to Costco or Target. We didn't need to spend $200 a month on hair, nails, and other beauty salon services.

We went back to basics. We stopped going to the store without a list. We agreed on an absolute minimum amount of cash that we would need. Every month we withdrew that amount of cash; ATM withdrawals were forbidden, and you know what? Simply examining these expenses allowed us to cut minor expenses to save major dollars.

Now that we are out of Hell, we are using our newfound savings to fund our daughter's education costs. My goal is to pay for her education, in its entirety, through these savings.

Investment Knowledge

Know how to spot opportunities. To thrive in times of change and economic uncertainty requires in-depth knowledge of investments and money. Write down where you feel your investment knowledge is strongest and the areas (such as accounting or charting) where you are weak.

Excess Cash

If your 401(k) is being maximized, the pressure of retirement savings is minimized. If you are regularly adding to your intermediate-term and long-term jar and are on track based on what is necessary to accomplish your goals, you are within striking position. When times get rough, you have these assets to be used for making solid investment decisions. You are consistently investing through all market cycles. These swords will all but ensure financial success.

A rule of thumb is that after all expenses are paid (including paying yourself), you should have an extra 10 percent left over. If you are able to attain this position, you have yet another strength.

STRIKES

Bad Debt

I talked previously about debt being a potential sword when used properly. I believe most successful people have had to use debt in some form or another. Prudent use of debt is OK. Credit card debt is never OK. You never, ever should borrow money for anything unless the interest rate is lower than the amount your capital is earning after taxes. This means that a bank's offer of a 1 percent car loan is good debt, because the money you would have used to pay for the car would be earning far more than 1 percent.

A second mortgage on your house (hard cash), credit card debt, and department store debt—all are bad debts. You need to be able to pay off your bills every month. Cut every expense except what is mandatory.

Variable Expenses

When you don't budget, variable expenses inevitably go up. Without a list for the grocery store, you are going to spend more than necessary. Budget for your big purchases and only make them when the time is right. Decide how much will be spent on entertainment, lunches, and the like.

If this is a problem, write it down as a strike. Understand that if you can live your lifestyle and have 10 percent left over, have a good time. Spend extra money. But only after you have an extra 10 percent left over. The objective is to have fun; and yet the two goals must check and balance one another to get you where you want to be—more prosperous while enjoying the journey.

Taxes

I have never known the IRS to say, "Hey, why don't you pay us a little less this year, Ken." Taxes are dollars that go out and never come back. The government must learn how to manage tax revenues better. To help them do that, I use every technique I can to take advantage of the system as it is written and minimize my taxes as much as possible.

In a nutshell, you and I pay a multitude of taxes: *income, sales, property, capital gains, estate, sin,* and *state taxes* to name a few. Some of these taxes can be controlled, minimized, or eliminated. As part of your personal wealth plan and as one of your largest combined fixed and variable expenses, you must audit your taxes. Compare your lifestyle and expenses with the income taxes you pay. After studying the correlation between how you spend your money, how much you spend, and how your various sources of income compare with the type and amount of taxes you pay, you should create a tax plan to reduce this expense.

Lack of Focus and Direction

Paying taxes with no knowledge of how to reduce them and going through life without a focused plan are both serious strikes that will hinder your growth.

Create your personal wealth plan, stick to it, and enjoy life!

BUILDING YOUR PERSONAL WEALTH PLAN

Everyone should create and adhere to a step-by-step plan for achieving financial goals in life. The plan should include a budget, savings plan, investment discipline, and desired outcome. Even though people have been exposed to financial plans in the past, one of the ways my plan differs is in its recommendation of different strategies under different economic conditions.

Review your shields, swords, and strikes. Work toward increasing your swords and decreasing your strikes.

Line up your short-term, intermediate-term, and long-term goals, and make certain your savings and investment plan is consistent with these goals.

What is a typical day? What is a typical week? What are the most important things in that week? What are the most enjoyable?

List capital, list expenses, list time constraints. Where do you have the most knowledge? Invest in what you know. Goals: what is your life's ambition? Which expenses are a must (pay yourself first) and which expenses can be cut?

RULE Plan to have an extra $1 million in 25 years.

Step One

As I discussed in Chapter 1, autopilot investing is key. A little bit invested every month will compound into a handsome sum. Albert Einstein stated that compound interest is the eighth wonder of the world—I agree. When interest compounds, it builds—and builds fast.

Let's go back to the assumption that you can average 12 percent compounded returns on your autopiloted long-term growth assets. (Remember there are no guarantees that you *can* obtain 12 percent compounded returns. There will be times when your return will be lower and there may be times when it is higher.) Let's assume that your family has a gross income of $70,000. Ten percent is $7,000, so if $7,000 compounded for 25 years equals $1 million. If you then retire and invest more conservatively, you might earn 8 percent, which gives you $80,000 per year. Not bad!

Now I don't want to hear that you don't have $7,000 per year. You do. Cut the frivolous expenses. Learn about your spending habits and then cut your taxes. You can do it! (See Figure 3.2.)

Rule of 72

Divide 72 by your interest rate. The result tells you approximately how long it will take your money to double. Seventy-two divided by 4 equals 18 years. Seventy-two divided by 12 equals 6 years.

___
RULE Maximize your budget-income ratio

Step Two

Under the paragraphs on swords, I stated it was prudent to be able to come in 10 percent under budget, which means that after all is said and done, including paying yourself first, you should have 10 percent of your gross income left over.

Assume you need $30,000 a year to live, including paying taxes; in addition, you determine you need an additional $300 a month to accomplish your intermediate-term and long-term goals. Your total expenses equal $33,600. Your income is $50,000 (gross). Clearly, you should have more than 10 percent of your income to sock away somewhere after all your expenses are paid. The first question is, where does the extra $16,400 go? Do you have it or has it evaporated? Did the savings get properly allocated to your intermediate-term and long-term jar?

As you will recall, the bottom of the cookie jar is money you won't need for ten years or more. If you know that this money won't be needed, it is prudent to strive for long-term growth and any tax savings that could be realized.

Ken Stern's School of Common Sense forbids you to move to Step Three until your goals are being properly funded. So be sure you are on track with your savings and investment plan. If you are on track with this plan, did you pay taxes on the $16,400 excess? The sign of a truly tax-efficient plan is that taxes are minimized, delayed, or avoided for excess income. You may consider various strategies for minimizing the tax consequences: tax-deferred retirement plans, increased deductions, investing in municipal bonds, or municipal bond funds.

Always strive to minimize the taxes in your intermediate-term and long-term jars.

LET'S CHAT ABOUT YOUR SPENDING PLAN

Throughout the slowdown/recession that our economy experienced beginning in 2000, people still borrowed and spent money— lots of money. Sales of big-ticket items, such as cars, barely hiccuped. I have two rules regarding spending and making money. First, it is essential to understand your spending personality. Second, pay yourself first. Since we just discussed the concept of paying yourself first (autopilot investing), let's focus on spending.

Your Spending Personality

Everyone has a spending personality. The sooner you learn yours, the easier it will be to save money and accomplish the second goal of paying yourself first.

Assume your spending personality is that of an *impulse buyer*— you *have* to buy things; it's a need, which means you have no premeditated buying plans. You see something, you like it, you buy it. If you could convince yourself to leave the store and wait to come back and buy it next week, 90 percent of the time you wouldn't purchase the item.

Some people have the spending personality of an *esteem buyer.* These people have a need to keep up with the Joneses. But you'll have more money than they do, you'll have a better plan, and you'll be able to retire sooner and stay retired longer. Forget what the Joneses have.

RULE Spend less by creating a budget.

One of the best ways to spend less is to create a budget. Start by carrying with you, everywhere you go, a pocket-sized pad of paper. Write down every single item you buy and expense you incur. The simple act of logging your expenses will shame you into reducing your expenses. You may find the coffee you buy every day is too expensive. Your car may eat too much gas, so you find a more fuel-efficient car. If you find that TV isn't that important, a $30 cable bill is a waste of money.

My commonsense money-saving ideas include these:

- Cut cable TV options.
- Buy a more fuel-efficient car.
- Pack your lunches.
- Cut your tax bill (I'll bet you can).
- Quit smoking.
- Buy in bulk.
- Wash your own car.
- Give gift certificates for things you can do instead of buying presents.

- Dine out less.
- Shop at discount stores.

Making a Game of Your Budget

Once you write down all of your expenses for a one-month period, create a budget. The start of your budget is the 10 percent you
pay yourself first. You then go through, line item by line item, what
you will spend on gifts, food, entertainment, electricity, and so on.
The best part about adhering to this budget is the monthly family
budget meetings you'll have. Every month the entire family gets together and discusses where you were under your budget and where
you were over your budget.

Reward yourself. Decide what you will do with the budget savings
after either a six-month period or a one-year period—then do it. You
could decide to take a trip or buy a boat. Treat yourself! As you track
how close you are to accomplishing your budget savings goal, everyone will get into it and become excited. It might be fun to do without cable for a while. If the heating bill gets too high, you may decide
to lower the heat and pile on the blankets.

The other day my wife and I went to work out. Coincidentally, we
both were wearing a new pair of shoes. I complimented her shoes
and she mine. I asked how much her shoes cost, to which she replied
$75. In a flash I thought of all the investments we could make for $75.
She asked how much I paid, and I stated $19. Obviously my wife and
I think differently about spending money!

▬▬▬
RULE Get prepared for early wealth.

Step Three

You now have everything in place to ensure early wealth. Your
savings are in place; your budget is kept tight. Your taxes are minimized. You are a lean, mean money machine.

Now's the time to call on your strengths to obtain early wealth.
You're in a position to be a bit more aggressive. If that extra 10 percent of your income, after expenses, is actually left over, you will have
a golden stash. You might use this to further implement the strategies
I've discussed. If we have already agreed you could amass $1 million

in 25 years, this extra stash, with prudent planning and investing, could cut that goal by half.

RULE Gather investment knowledge and begin implementing your investment plan.

Ken Stern's School of Common Sense now allows you to learn how to invest and create an investment plan. Remember that the best investors stick to this plan through thick and thin. It takes discipline and courage. You are ready.

SUMMARY

Your personal wealth plan is in place. You know what it's going to take. The rest is fun. Stick to your personal wealth plan. Stick to your budget. Keep your golden stash ready for opportunities as they present themselves. When they surface, carefully assess the situation, but don't be afraid to pounce.

The next time you are propositioned or are considering making a large purchase or any investment, ask yourself what the risk-versus-reward ratio is.

It sure is a great feeling to know that if all else fails, you should be able to weather the downturn, have a ready arsenal of strengths, and not be thrown through a loop by unforeseen events. And if nothing else, you should be a millionaire in 25 years.

CHAPTER FOUR

It's Time to Gather Acorns and Build Your Personal Board of Directors

"Strength does not come from winning. Your struggles develop your strengths. When you go through hardships and decide not to surrender, that is strength." —Arnold Schwarzenegger

The reason most people can't take advantage of a market in an economic downturn is that very few commit to a plan. The personal wealth plan is your plan. Regardless of what analogy I use—rain or acorns—the point is the same. Prepare for the downturn. It is coming and you should be in a position to profit from it.

Remember your strengths and your swords. When the downturn comes, make sure that your strengths are plentiful, and your strikes are few.

Identify the areas you feel you are best positioned to exploit and capitalize on.

One of the best ways to create wealth is to be ready and able to pounce on opportunity when it comes. A slowdown in the economy is one of the best opportunities that is both a regular occurrence and available to everyone.

Well before the downturn, it's a good idea to prepare. Even though I got caught in the early stages of the down cycle, it was the preparations I had previously made that allowed me to get out of Hell faster. Those preparations I can share with you in the form of the following six commonsense (gathering acorns) tips:

1. Be free of bad debt.
2. Have direct access to capital.
3. Create research lists.
4. Get educated and network.
5. Create your board of directors.
6. Continue to gather acorns.

BE FREE OF DEBT, INCREASE SAVINGS, AND HAVE ACCESS TO CAPITAL

I must be crazy. First I say you need to be debt free, and then I say you must have access to capital. Allow me to explain.

Early on I learned that leverage was the way to build a fortune faster then you could think possible. I have also seen debt bankrupt people in the blink of an eye. Based on the risks versus the rewards, this is the philosophy I adopted: Consumer debt is absolutely forbidden. Regardless of the debt's being from a credit card, furniture, or even medical work, you may not borrow money and pay interest on any purchase unless that purchase (investment) has the possibility of appreciating.

RULE Ken Stern's School of Common Sense forbids you to have any revolving/consumer debt (other than your home and maybe your car).

I know we just covered the importance of savings in the previous chapter. But this is the most important rule I can share with you. As much as I love talking about investing, do you know what common ingredient the wealthy share? They save more than they spend. That's it. They respect and understand money. They don't borrow from investments such as 401(k) plans. They don't borrow money for clothes or any other depreciating want. Regardless of your income, you can and must save money.

To further drive home this point, consider the chart in Figure 4.1. It shows that the savings rate among consumers in the United States has now dipped into negative territory (2 percent). Granted, this does not count investments, but it still clearly illustrates that the savings rate has dropped to an unacceptable level over the last several years. Spend less then you make. Your goal is to save at 8 to 10 percent of your gross income.

FIGURE 4.1   The Personal Savings Rate

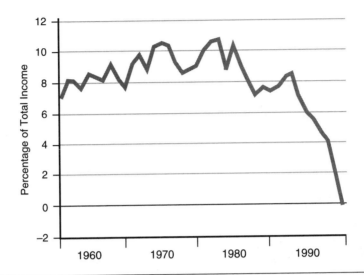

Early on in my professional life, I used credit cards. I insisted when times were good, however, that everything would be sacrificed until they were paid off. I didn't spend money on lunches, movies, or cable TV until those bills were paid off. This is a critical stage in gathering acorns. If you have problems with credit card debt, immediately go to a credit counselor!

At the same time, I established credit for investment purposes by networking with bankers. As the relationships grew, I negotiated favorable credit lines and small loans. These were not intended to be used right away, nor did I pay interest unless I used them. I opened a brokerage account and made sure margin was available (although I didn't use it).

When the downturn came and deals presented themselves, I did (and will in the future) use debt when and if I felt the debt to be for an excellent investment. I wouldn't borrow large amounts as others did. Perhaps 20 percent to 25 percent debt-to-total assets would not be out of line. I wouldn't use all the debt in one place. Whether it's real estate or stocks and regardless of the

Debt-to-Total Assets Ratio. Total liabilities divided by total capital. Divide your assets by your debt and you have your personal debt-equity ratio.

amount of research you do, you will not always pick winners. So when the downturn came, I made sure to spread the risk.

CREATE A RESEARCH LIST

Let's assume you knew nothing about investing. But you knew intuitively that when recessions come or stock markets crash, investments (in general) get cheaper. Go buy yourself a three-ring binder. Separate the binder with ten dividers, each section representing your research for a different company.

Try to choose companies from different industries to research. Food, apparel, energy, software, semiconductors, utilities, pharmaceuticals, biotechnology, retailers, airlines, financial services, and hotels are a few examples. However, pay special attention to those companies in the industry (or industries) you understand.

Create a graph of the price performance of various companies' stock. You can either plot the graph yourself or download a graph from one of the popular Web sites that has graphs. Get onto the companies' Web sites once a month and record any new or interesting facts. Call different brokerages and ask them to send you new research material on these companies as they come due. Many Web sites allow you to track stocks as well. If there is any news on such a company, you'll be alerted. Even ask the shareholder service department to e-mail you as press releases are published.

The objective, the desired outcome, of all this research and tracking is for you to become familiar with patterns.

If news about the economy, interest rates, or retail spending is announced (see Chapter 6), how do the stocks in your research group react? Do they tend to react the same every time a similar report is released? How does a stock do after the company announces its quarterly earnings? How did it do a week before and a week after? Do you like the tone of the management's letters and correspondence with the public? Is there a trend of high employee turnover? Do you see a company gaining or losing market share? Log any information that you may find helpful. Even if you are analyzing a particular restaurant but find that the manager wasn't friendly and the restaurant wasn't busy, log it! Go to stores. Ask the people working on the floor if they are getting pressure from management to sell more and if business has been slow. Look for patterns.

Understand that this is research. It is very basic and does not qualify you for the stock picker's hall of fame, but I do believe that you will have an excellent overview of certain patterns that develop. This knowledge will undoubtedly help you understand a company and the behavior of the company's stock during various economic cycles.

IT'S ALL ABOUT EDUCATION AND NETWORKING

Persistence, discipline, and *knowledge* are the three most important ingredients for success. Knowledge is a never-ending quest gained through both traditional education and experience.

Read books and biographies of those who are successful. Attend classes and go to meetings. If some of the accounting terms I present are complicated, take a class that teaches you about accounting as it relates to securities analysis.

Many valuable classes and groups exist; research the best ones for you. Though incomplete, the following are some of the organizations I personally found helpful.

Investment Clubs

Imagine regular people forming a club to talk about investing and then to invest. Many of these groups ante up a very small amount of money, with everyone pooling their funds to buy a few stocks. Your friends are counting on you, so you had better bring a well-researched stock idea for the next meeting. Investment clubs are a terrific, inexpensive way to learn.

If you are going to have an investment club, do it right. Have guest speakers—analysts or officers of corporations that you are investing in. Many clubs join an association called the National Association of Investors Corporation (NAIC). The NAIC is a nonprofit, largely volunteer organization dedicated to investor education that I recommend you join. Although the Securities and Exchange Commission (SEC) prohibits the NAIC from helping you find an investment club to join, it does make regional club information available. Most regional clubs invite potential members to attend meetings. The NAIC has a great Web site, and membership includes a handbook on mutual funds and a monthly investment magazine. Membership costs vary from $20 for a youth membership to $575

*National Association of Investors Corporation
711 W. 13 Mile Road
Madison Heights, MI 48071
877-275-6242
<www.better-investing.com>*

for a lifetime individual membership (at this writing, annual individual dues were $39).

New York Institute of Finance

New York Institute of Finance
800-227-NYIF (6943)
212-641-6616
<www.nyif.com>
info@nyif.com

The New York Institute of Finance offers short classes and seminars on a variety of subjects, all of them dealing with investing, stock selection, accounting, and economics. Most of the classes are geared more to practical application than to abstract theory; and some classes are offered online. The institute's U.S. offices are in New York, Boston, and San Francisco.

American Association of Individual Investors

American Association of Individual Investors
625 N. Michigan Avenue
Chicago, IL 60611
800-428-2244
<www.aaii.com>

This group is another excellent resource for individual investors. Knowledgeable guest speakers and enlightening research are presented at regular meetings. The association also publishes a well thought-out newsletter that is filled with useful information.

Various Educationally Oriented Investment Web Sites

There are many useful Web sites that can help you learn more about investments, plan your financial future, and track your portfolio.

YOUR NEW BOARD OF DIRECTORS

In many cases, experience is even more valuable than education. Creating mock portfolios, asking questions, and being observant can all pay off handsomely. Our world is the greatest classroom. Use it. When the slowdown comes, education can give you a vital edge.

Hand in hand with education is networking. Networking can introduce you to analysts, employers, accountants, bankers, attorneys, and, most important, people who are simply part of the "food" chain.

Some people work with or at companies that are usually early to see economic changes coming. A company that leads the economic cycle might feel a slowdown before other industries but also begin growing again while growth in other industries is still slow. Your friends work for other companies. These companies may or may not be doing well. They may have favorite suppliers and companies they sell to.

The best networking you can do is surround yourself with those who are going to facilitate your goal. These people I call your board of directors.

Team of Advisors

"Two heads are better then one" is usually a true statement. When it comes to money, the more people you have feeding you good ideas, the better. The key is to make sure the ideas are viable and that you have enough knowledge to distinguish good advice from a sack of potatoes.

Regardless of whether you are in the accumulation phase of your wealth journey or in the maintenance or disposition phase, a forward-thinking, smart, honest group of advisors—a board of directors—will be a critical part of your journey. You are the chairman, and you now fill the board with key components.

One critical aspect is that these advisors must talk to one another. Far too often, the certified public accountant doesn't talk to the attorney, and the attorney doesn't talk to the financial planner, which possibly leads to oversights and gaps in advice.

Financial Planners

I like to think that the financial planner should act as the president of your board. Because I've worked as a financial advisor for so many years, my assumption may be biased. However, a good planner acts as the master of ceremonies, overseeing your financial well-being.

First and foremost, a comprehensive plan needs to be created based on the personal wealth formula. A worthwhile financial plan should both raise and answer key questions. For example, common-sense questions a financial planner should ask:

- What amount of income do you currently use?
- How do you spend your time—that is, what do you like to do?
- How do you spend your money?

- Is your CPA aware of these activities and, as a result, maximizing all possible deductions?
- Is your estate plan created to ensure that wealth is maximized and passed on properly?
- Whom do you want to have control of your wealth if you cannot control it?
- Do you want to leave your wealth to your heirs or spend your last dollar in your last days?

A financial advisor should help you answer the previous questions as well as questions that haven't yet been formulated:

- You should be clear about how much money you will need to live comfortably throughout your life without worrying about money.
- Ideas should be introduced on how to cut budget expenses (including taxes).
- Suggestions for the other advisors on how to coordinate a joint effort to make more money for you, pay a lesser amount in taxes, and increase your asset protection.
- Ideas for creating a plan to ensure that your goals are achieved with the minimal asset risk.

For the most part, think of your financial planner as the facilitator. He or she probably doesn't actually manage the money but should do more than simply run a few reports to determine who *should* manage your money. I've found that many people manage their money by going to a popular Web site, printing out historical data on a stock or mutual fund, and, based solely on returns, deciding how to invest their funds. Danger! Danger!

Investing solely on historical performance is a terrible way to choose who will manage your funds. You don't know the risk associated with future returns, how that particular investment is positioned for today's market environment, or the competency of the current management to match those historical returns.

Choosing a financial planner could be a bit tricky. As with all businesses, good and bad practitioners exist. Methods of compensation differ greatly throughout the industry, and different planners have different levels of education.

When considering a planner, the following suggestions may be helpful. Seek referrals from CPAs and attorneys. Some financial planners have obtained the Certified Financial Planner (CFP) designation from the College for Financial Planning, a private industry group that seeks to educate and regulate the planning industry.

Once you have at least three names, interview the planners. First, you need to ascertain exactly what services will be rendered. Is this planner going to review your entire life, create the plan, and ask the questions discussed above? If you manage your own money (or part of it), will the planner monitor this as well as your 401(k), along with the assets the planner is assigned to directly watch over? Does the planner create a plan as well as make investment recommendations? Ask about the planner's educational background, and request any recently created sample plans that you could review.

When reviewing a sample plan, determine if it addresses all the above questions. Of course, call as many references as possible. When calling references, ask how long they have been with the planner, how well they know the planner, and what the planner's strengths and weaknesses are.

Most financial planners are registered with the National Association of Securities Dealers (NASD), a self-regulatory organization much like a state bar association for attorneys. You can research your financial planner and stockbroker—and the firms they are associated with—either by writing the NASD or accessing its Web site at <www.nasdr.com>. Click on "About Your Broker," where you are given the options of an online search or downloading a form to request the information in writing. Another option is an online review of the planner's or broker's current employment; previous employment (ten years); approved registrations (for brokers and for firms); address information; types of business conducted; legal status; and a public disclosure report for either if it exists. The public disclosure report contains information about any violations of securities regulations, arrests, significant employment information (such as terminations for cause), or any significant customer complaints. Unfortunately, you cannot ask specific questions of the NASD regarding a registered representative or a firm. However, if you have a complaint about either one, you can write to your regional NASD office.

If you would rather call than visit the Web site, you can request the information through the NASD Regulation's Public Disclosure toll-free number: 800-289-9999. The request is generally processed within two business days but may take longer.

> **N**ational Association of
> Securities Dealers, Inc.
> 800-289-9999
> <www.nasdr.com>

Fees. Once this review is accomplished, you can discuss fees. Planners are usually compensated in one of two ways: commissions or on the basis of fees.

It is important for you, the client, to know if your planner is commission oriented. I have no problem with a planner making money; I just want to know what incentive the planner has to make money for me. What is the motivation to make moves in the account? Is it for another commission or because the financial plan calls for a change? Compensation can often go beyond commissions. Sometimes a planner may receive an incentive trip for selling a product. Ask whether the company issuing the product the planner is selling offers incentive trips; you want to know if the planner is using a product to qualify for a sales trip. Commissioned salespeople realize that if you aren't happy, you aren't going to stay with them. If you jump ship, there go the commissions, so they have an incentive to make you happy.

Fee planners, on the other hand, are not supposed to make any money for investment recommendations. They are paid a fee to create and implement a plan. This payment method can benefit the client because moves in an account are not made to generate commissions. Nonetheless, I would ask the same questions. How often is the account being monitored? Are fees assessed when changes are made in the investment allocation or the financial plan? Are you going to have to pay the planner a fee and a broker a commission to implement any trades?

Fees as a percentage of assets. One common method of payment is to charge a fee as a percentage of assets managed. As the planner grows the assets, the client has accumulated more wealth for the planner to manage, so the planner's fee grows in direct proportion to the growth in assets that the client enjoys.

Money Managers

AIMR. *Association for Investment Management and Research sets standards for reporting performance. If a fund is AIMR compliant, the manager has conformed to the standards.*

Whether you are using a financial planner to find your money manager(s) or are finding the money manager yourself, certain questions must be asked. Let's start with the premise that there are two methods of investing in equities: mutual funds and individual equities.

Individual money management. Most individual money managers are regulated and registered as a Registered Investment

Advisor (RIA). If they manage over $25 million, they must be registered with the Securities & Exchange Commission (as opposed to being registered only in the states where they do business).

All money managers should be able to provide the following information (in writing):

- Track record
- Investment style
- Investment objective
- How portfolio investments are selected
- How long the current investment managers have been at the fund and their experience level
- If they are AIMR compliant
- If they are a CFA (Chartered Financial Analyst) in good standing
- Risk inherent in their style
- Whether they will implement tax strategies
- What their fee structure is and if there are hidden fees within their funds

Certified Public Accountant (CPA)

A CPA can be either a lifesaver or a bookkeeper. Let's start with the latter. Many CPAs simply prepare tax returns. Their fee is paid to organize your papers, extract the data provided, transfer these data to the appropriate tax form, and complete the return. Please make no mistake—this is paying someone to prepare your taxes. It is not a tax plan.

On the other hand, a true tax planner is adding more value than simply preparing a return. A tax planner gets to know you, your lifestyle, and your spending and investing habits. A tax planner talks to your other board members to determine different strategies to maximize your estate and minimize unnecessary tax burdens. (See the chapter on shields, swords, and strikes.)

Where to find good tax advisors. CPAs are regulated at the state level. Most states have two organizations that should be able to help you locate a CPA. One is an organization of CPAs, such as the California Society of CPAs. The other is the state regulatory body, usually called the board of accountancy. At a minimum, a board of accountancy can verify that a person does hold a CPA license in that state. Some state Web sites (for instance, California's) give more detailed information, such as whether a CPA has received any disciplinary actions.

Stockbrokers

The role of a stockbroker is ever changing. Traditionally, a stockbroker would buy and sell a stock on behalf of his or her client. Now, many types of brokers exist.

Full-service brokers. A full-service broker is one who buys and sells stocks and bonds on your behalf for a commission but also provides added services. The commission is typically higher than that of a discount broker. The added services that justify the higher commission could vary from providing advice to sending the client stock research, from providing access to checking accounts to, in some cases, financial planning services. A few conflicts of interest may surface.

If a broker recommends you buy a stock, be certain you understand whether the company of the stock recommended is a client of the brokerage company. Often, brokerage companies provide research on companies that they do business with in other capacities, such as banking or consulting. Imagine how awkward it would be if XYZ Brokerage were to have a client called Ken's Widgets. Imagine if XYZ were to tell its brokers, through a research report, that Ken's Widgets stinks and that the stock is a sell. I doubt Ken's Widgets would be a client of XYZ for very long!

In addition, further potential conflicts of interest arise from commissions. It's OK to buy and sell stocks—if there is a rationale and a plan. You want to know what the rationale and plan are before simply buying and selling. The concern is to be sure that the broker is not making trades solely to make higher commissions on your account.

I have seen a trend where brokers don't manage the money themselves. Instead, the broker finds money managers (either individual or mutual funds) who will charge a fee for managing the assets. The broker gets an ongoing fee based on the amount of money invested for as long as the account is maintained. In some ways, this may be a fairer way to be compensated, as the potential conflict of interest of buying and selling doesn't exist.

Discount brokers. Until 2000, it looked as though the discount broker concept would continue to gain in popularity to the point that a majority of Americans would use discount brokers in some capacity. More and more people thought that investing was as easy as pie (whatever that means), so why should they pay a full-service broker when they could do it themselves? Then came the bear market. Many investors got caught and lost vast sums of money. We saw a decline in the number of new discount accounts being opened. In a traditional discount brokerage account, investors do their own research. If research services were provided, the fee would be higher. To stay competitive, many companies have begun to increase support to their clients, including research. With the advent of the Internet, many companies have allowed trades to be placed directly online; still others permit trades through either the Internet or the telephone.

An investor should have answers to many questions regarding a relationship with a discount broker. First, the investor needs to understand the solvency of the company and how financially secure it is. People often assume their money is secure simply because it is with a brokerage firm. This may not be the case. Assume you were to deposit $20,000 into a brokerage account in anticipation of buying stocks at some point. How secure is the cash in the brokerage account? If the brokerage company deposits the funds in its proprietary money market, how safe is that money market fund? Is the money market allowed to invest in noncredit quality or nonrated securities?

Broker-dealers are required to be members of the Securities Investor Protection Corporation (SIPC), which provides insurance to the customers of failed broker-dealers. Although SIPC cannot protect a customer from fluctuations in the market, the SIPC will appoint a trustee to ensure that all securities registered in the client's name are properly distributed if a broker-dealer fails financially. After satisfying customer claims with available company funds, SIPC dollars are used to ensure that each client is made whole to a maximum of $500,000 per client. This $500,000 includes $100,000 in cash held by the broker-dealer. You can verify that a broker-dealer is a SIPC member by visiting its Web site at <www.sipc.org>.

> *S*ecurities Investor
> Protection Corporation
> 805 15th Street NW,
> Suite 800
> Washington, DC 20005
> 202-371-8300
> <www.sipc.org>

Another concern is the quality of the execution.

RULE When you trade a stock or a bond, you want to make sure that the trade is executed in a timely manner and that you get a good execution price.

I have heard horror stories of people calling a brokerage firm to place a trade and then being placed on hold long enough to play a round of golf. I am exaggerating, of course, but delays can and will affect the outcome of your trades. This is because a stock can move a lot between the time you wished to place the trade and when you actually were able to place it. The same happens to people who place their trades through the Internet. Sometimes the trade does not get executed in a timely manner.

The other concern, which could actually be of more importance, is how well your trade is executed. Most investors know there is a difference between the price the public pays and the price that professionals pay. You want to be absolutely certain you are getting the best price possible. Toward this effort, two exercises could be helpful.

The first is to simply ask the brokerage company how trades are executed. Do they shop your trade for a better price? Do they buy your stock directly or do they resell you stock that they may already have in their inventory? Exactly what is the commission you will be charged? If the trade was filled at $10.00 per share, does your brokerage company add on $.25, giving it to you for $10.25 and pocketing the extra $25.00 on a 100-share transaction? Ask, too, if the brokerage firm makes a market in the stock, which means it will receive a portion of the spread or commission, and you may be able to negotiate.

Over the last several years, the exchanges that trade stocks (such as the Nasdaq and the New York Stock Exchange) have done a very good job of minimizing the spread between stocks. I believe this has been instrumental in helping even smaller investors get a fair price on their stock trades. So be careful about execution and about hidden fees and markups, such as those described above.

Finally, be careful about add-on fees and risks. Do additional fees exist when you withdraw money or if you close your account? Is there an additional fee for each account statement you receive?

Commonsense online trading questions you should ask include the following:

- What are the fees and expenses?
- Are the stocks marked up?
- Is there a transfer fee?
- Is there a minimum amount necessary to open the account or a minimum number of trades to open an account or get the rates quoted?
- Is opening the account on margin a requirement?
- What is the insurance coverage provided for assets held in cash reserves? Is there an amount over the minimum SIPC insurance?
- Is trading on margin a requirement?

- Is there any written material describing how quickly a trade is executed once it is made? On average, how long is a client placed on hold?
- What types of research and guidance services are available?
- Can you also own certificates of deposit, mutual funds (load or no-load), options, stocks, bonds, and bank accounts in this account? Is there any additional charge for these types of investments?

RESOURCES AND WATCH DOGS FOR INDIVIDUAL INVESTORS

National Association of Securities Dealers, Inc.

This excellent educational Web site offers information on brokers, complaint processes, investor alerts, and contact information for regional NASD offices. Some areas in this Web site are technical, but those specifically designed for investors are in easy-to-read everyday language.

> *National Association of Securities Dealers, Inc.*
> *800-289-9999*
> *<www.nasdr.com>*

Securities and Exchange Commission (SEC)

Again, much of this Web site is extremely technical and focused. However, the Investor Information section is easy to read and has a lot of valuable information.

> *Securities and Exchange Commission*
> *202-942-7040*
> *<www.sec.gov>*

North American Securities Administrators Association (NASAA)

NASAA is the oldest international organization devoted to investor protection. The Web site has some interesting articles on such topics as "Top 10 Investment Scams." The majority of the Web site is dedicated to contact information for the regulatory bodies

> *North American Securities Administrators Association, Inc.*
> *888-84NASAA*
> *(846-2722)*
> *<www.nasaa.org>*

in the 50 states, Washington, D.C., Puerto Rico, Canada, and Mexico. This site is a gold mine of information on other important industry Web sites and contact information.

American Association of Individual Investors (AAII)

American Association of Individual Investors
800-428-2244
<www.aaii.com>

This site has some interesting and informative articles. To access most of the information available, membership in the AAII is required.

Certified Financial Planner Board of Standards

Certified Financial Planner Board of Standards
303-830-7500
<www.cfp-board.org>

This site has easy-to-read articles on some of the topics covered in this book, such as checking out a broker and filing a complaint.

IT'S TIME FOR A BOARD MEETING

On average, I meet with the various members of my board once per quarter individually; and every year we all get together as a group. I send an agenda to them, and they prepare for the meeting accordingly. They know that other professionals (the other members of my board of directors) will scrutinize their report.

The CPA not only discusses my tax return but also various tax-saving ideas that are being implemented. The financial planner simply answers the financial planning questions that are posed. The money manager talks about the year and how well it went.

If you feel the business cycle will be experiencing a major shift, either from peak to contraction or from trough to expansion, you need to call a special board meeting. The agenda is simple: how are we going to prepare, protect, and profit through the change.

SUMMARY

Only fools rush in. The rest of us gather acorns. Those who don't gather acorns are going to have a hard time eating when it rains or in the winter. Think of a recession like winter.

The best part about gathering acorns is, like money, you never stop gathering. While I was in Hell, desperately trying to escape, I was still gathering acorns. The most valuable acorns I gathered were education (which you are always gathering), networking (which should be an ongoing effort that is increased during the bad times), and building or improving your board of directors. If we are in a downturn now, some aspects, such as getting out of debt, are harder to accomplish and even harder when trying to decide if you want to invest or pay off debt. Nevertheless, consumer debt is strictly forbidden regardless of the economic cycle.

I hope it is absolutely clear that the information and steps provided in these first four chapters are as critical to investment success, to thriving during the downturn, as any other knowledge you may possess. Unfortunately, not much attention is usually paid to these techniques. Without your board, you are a one-man show. It's dark and scary during the slowdown.

The Economy
and the
Business Cycle

PART TWO

The Key to
Great Investing

CHAPTER FIVE

The Business Cycle:
Your Treasure Map

Becoming a world-class investor takes four broad skills: (1) determining which phase of the business cycle we're in; (2) finding the sectors that will perform best during each phase of the business cycle; (3) understanding how to value a company within that sector; and (4) possessing the discipline, savvy, and moxie to stick with your plan.

Look at the depiction of the business cycle in Figure 5.1. Read it. Study it. Relish it. If you can conquer the business cycle, you're 25

FIGURE 5.1 The Business Cycle

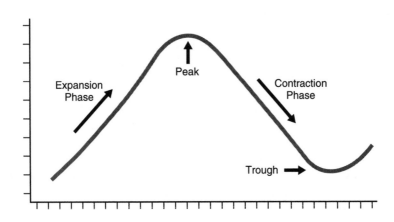

percent closer to Nirvana—world-class investing. Now you just need to match the proper sector based on the business cycle and use your stock-picking skills to find the right stock.

Had I not stopped monitoring the business cycle, I doubt I would have gone to Hell during 2000. However, after reading the business cycle tea leaves, I returned to my discipline and found a quick exit from the gates of Hell!

If I were you, I would take a copy of the business cycle (Figure 5.1), enlarge it, and frame it. It might be one of the most valuable swords in your arsenal.

Please do not confuse the business cycle with the stock market. In fact, when the economy is at its best, the stock market, as you will learn, may be crashing, and vice versa. We need to know about the business cycle for investing, however, like most things in life, investments are influenced by general environmental conditions that need to be considered. It's important to have an understanding of the business cycle to determine which factors will most heavily impact your individual investments.

WHAT IS THE BUSINESS CYCLE?

The business cycle is defined by the recurring periods of expansion (recovery) and contraction (recession) that occur in our economy. A recession is generally considered to be two successive quarters of decline in the real gross domestic product (GDP). Recovery, or expansion, is identified by rising output, consumption, and employment. Expansion and contraction can be affected by inflation, production, and employment. Periods of expansion eventually reach a peak, whereas periods of recession ultimately enter a trough. In the event a recession is prolonged, the economy enters into a depression.

This is what happens—in a six-point nutshell:

1. The economy is in a recession/neorecession.
2. The Federal Reserve lowers interest rates to pump cash into the economy and increase liquidity in the economy.
3. Increased cash and liquidity support financial markets and, in turn, allow corporate balance sheets to improve. Consumer debt stabilizes and banks become more solvent.
4. New orders and production take off. Profits recover, the stock market bottoms, inventories increase, and consumer expenditures rise.

5. Full capacity is reached: stock prices peak, inflation starts to take off, demand for funds pushes up real interest rates, and new economic excesses are created.
6. Banks withdraw liquidity, short-term interest rates rise, financial markets fall, the economy contracts, and economic excesses are eliminated.

EVERYTHING YOU NEED TO KNOW ABOUT ECONOMICS . . . BUT NO ONE CAN EXPLAIN (UNTIL NOW)

The U.S. economy, like all economies, is driven by demand and supply. At any given time, a certain number of goods and services are available in the marketplace with a certain supply of money and a certain number of consumers chasing these goods and services. These goods and services are the gross domestic product (GDP), the "market value of the goods and services produced by labor and property in the United States . . . made up of consumer and government purchases, private domestic investments, and net exports of goods and services. . . . Growth of the U.S. economy is measured by the change in inflation-adjusted GDP, or real GDP" *(Barron's Financial Guides Dictionary of Finance and Investment Terms).*

Our economy generally expands when consumers spend more money on goods and services. This increased demand allows manufacturers to produce more goods and services and raise the prices of available goods and services. As more goods and services are produced, more workers are required to produce them. Two things happen at this point: (1) Unemployment drops because more workers return to the workplace, and (2) workers are able to demand higher wages. During this phase, consumers and businesses borrow money, causing interest rates to rise. Inflation increases as the demand for goods and services overtakes the supply; the economy moves toward a peak. Inflation exists when there are not enough goods and services to satisfy the demand, allowing businesses to raise prices. The purchasing power of consumers is reduced because they cannot buy as much with the same dollar. As prices rise, consumers begin to forgo luxury items, and demand weakens. By the time demand begins to weaken, the economy moves into either the contractionary or the recessionary phase. Employers lay off workers, causing unemployment to increase. This further weakens demand, which causes the economy to slow or even reverse. The economy reaches a trough (see Figure 5.2).

FIGURE 5.2   The Business Cycle Trough

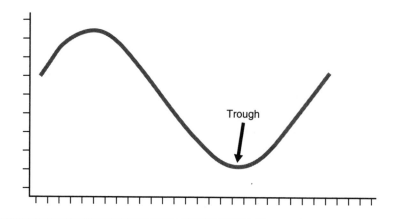

At some point, lower prices help stimulate demand and the economy enters an expansionary phase again.

THE PHASES OF THE BUSINESS CYCLE

Once we correctly define the phases of the business cycle, we can then attempt to define which assets tend to perform best during each phase of the cycle.

Stage One: The Trough

Characteristic indications of the trough are the following:

- Layoffs are peaking.
- Interest rates are being dropped aggressively, resulting in a steeper yield curve.
- Consumer confidence is low.
- Most economic indicators signal economic weakness.
- Pessimism is high.
- Unemployment is high.
- The stock market is probably down.
- The inflation rate is usually falling.

This is the bottom of the business, or economic, cycle. It may not feel like the bottom after having gone through what you just did (an economic contraction). At this stage in the cycle everything has fallen apart and the economy has just created an "L" pattern—a steep correction that is now leveling off.

It's hard to know specifically if the economy is still contracting or has, in fact, bottomed out. The money supply is very weak and it's harder to borrow money. Interest rates have dropped, probably several times in succession. Unemployment has already risen, and chances are that stocks are considered cheap on the basis of historical measures.

One of the reasons it may be difficult to tell if we are in a trough is the conflicting information you hear from so-called experts. Some experts might say, "Stocks are only cheap if the economy rebounds." Bankruptcies are so high that few are predicting an end to negative business conditions anytime soon.

Of course, the economy may not begin to expand soon. But to identify the trough, you want to look at your economic data. Right before the trough, the contraction probably experienced its worst point. Everything from unemployment to construction had probably gapped down. Immediately after this gap, economic activity remained slack. It's hoped that by this time, interest rates will have dropped enough to catch up with the slowing economy. Look for a steeper yield curve, which means that the spread between short-term and long-term interest rates has increased. Consider the yield curve in Figure 5.3. Notice that short-term interest rates are very low for lower maturities.

FIGURE 5.3   Yield Curve

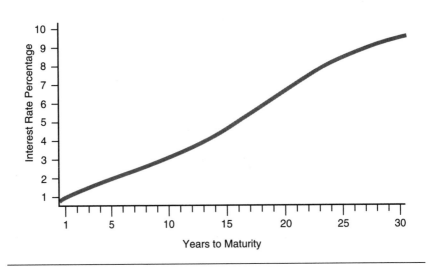

The higher the maturity, the higher the interest rate. This is a healthy yield curve and one you would see from a late contraction of the economic cycle all the way through an early expansion.

All of these indicators are signs that the economy has entered a trough. In addition, you may even see companies begin to state that orders for goods and services might pick up one or two quarters out.

Pay attention to the trough. Ironically, this is one of the best times to invest. I will show you why, during late April 2001, I believe the U.S. economy had entered a trough; and I show you in the chapter, "When in Doubt, Hedge Your Bets," the investments we made as a result.

Stage Two: Expansion

Just the name of the second stage of the business cycle should tell you this is a good time for the economy. Historically, the expansionary phase (see Figure 5.4) is the longest part of the business cycle. In fact, the entire expansion phase should be split into three parts: the early stage, the middle stage, and the late stage.

The Early Stage

The beginning of the expansion stage, the period when our economy is transitioning from a trough to expansion, is truly the filet. It's

FIGURE 5.4   The Business Cycle Expansion

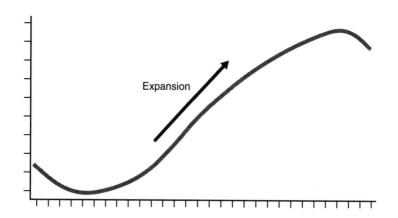

Expansion

the best time for companies as well as for investors. The early stage of expansion (see Figure 5.5) is characterized by the following:

- The rate of increase in companies' earnings is the highest.
- Inflation is low.
- Interest rates are low and have probably just experienced several rate reductions.
- Consumer confidence has stabilized or is possibly trending higher.
- Companies have trimmed excess and are extremely efficient.
- Most of the negative news has stabilized.
- The stock market may be spiking higher.

At first, it seems odd that this is the stage when earnings are increasing at the highest rate, but that's generally the case. We just completed a terrible contraction in the economy. Earnings of most companies were down. Many companies lost money. If a company in the previous contraction (say a year ago) lost $1.00 per share, and now it projects it will earn $2.00 a share, isn't that increasing its earnings by 100 percent? In the next year of the expansion (say the middle), it may even predict earnings of $2.20 per share. Although it's great that the company is now profitable and expanding its earnings, the percentage gain from $2.00 to $2.20 is only an incremental 10 percent gain. This may be considered positive because the company is expanding its earnings, but it is not expanding at the same rate of growth it was in the early stage of the expansion.

FIGURE 5.5   The Early Stage of Expansion

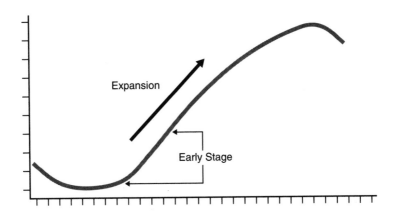

It also makes sense that companies are more efficient at this stage. Their workforces are streamlined (and wages are often lower), factories are run more efficiently, and the intermediate goods the factory buys are probably fairly inexpensive as well.

The Middle Stage

These are characteristic indications of the middle stage of expansion:

- Solid gains are seen in most sections of the economy.
- Short-term interest rates have probably stabilized and are no longer dropping sharply.
- Interest rates begin to trend higher.
- Businesses expand.
- Some inflation of goods and services can be noticed.
- Lower unemployment is seen.
- Growth stocks are achieving solid gains.

The middle stage of expansion (see Figure 5.6) is usually the longest part of the business cycle and is characterized as a happy time. When businesses expand, people go back to work. Retail sales, including big-ticket items, show excellent year-over-year gains. The slowdown in the economy is long forgotten and things are going too well to really think about another slowdown.

FIGURE 5.6   The Middle Stage of Expansion

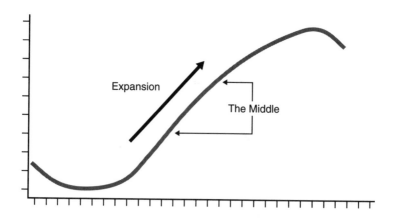

The Late Stage to the Peak

These are characteristic indicators of the late stage of expansion to the peak:

- Higher prices for goods and services—signs of inflation—are noticeable.
- Short-term interest rates may rise.
- Earnings are often the highest just before the end of the stage.
- Profit margins may begin to shrink.
- Confidence is extremely high.
- A recession is the furthest thing from anyone's mind.

Rates rise for two reasons. First, there is a large demand on companies to spend money. They need to build more factories and buy out competition, and they need money to produce more goods and services before they are ultimately sold.

When growth is so robust, inflation often follows. Inflation reduces the value of money, and nobody wants that. As a result, those that manage our economy are initially more concerned with inflationary speed rather than with a recession for obvious reasons.

To slow the rate of inflation, the Fed increases short-term interest rates to lower the money supply in an attempt to slow consumption and credit expansion.

But it's OK—only God could sink this ship! The good times are here and everyone is employed, spending money, and having a great time (see Figure 5.7).

Stage Three: The Peak

Characteristics of the peak include the following:

- Supply shortages are typical.
- Short-term interest rates rise and the yield curve flattens.
- Economic indicators remain high, even too high.
- The money supply is tightened in short order by the Fed.
- Stocks are overvalued relative to historic rates, and it's typical for sell-offs to increase at this point.
- Unemployment is low and wage price pressure is high.
- Silly stories run rampant.

FIGURE 5.7   The Late Stage—the Peak—of Expansion

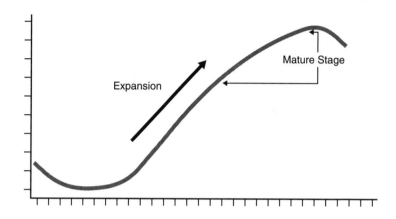

Businesses are booming—they can't hire fast enough. They are opening new plants. A recession is the last thing on people's minds, but when you see an incredible spike in shortages, it's coming.

One might think that a peak happens very quickly. Like a mountain, we climb to the top, reach it, and immediately start trending lower. As happened during 1999, the peak could be deceiving. Economists argue just how long our economy was at the peak. As for the stock market, even with impressive earnings recorded by many companies, stocks were historically considered overvalued—one sign of a peaking economy. We had incredible supply shortages in certain industries, such as semiconductors (computer chips). Interest rates increased several times in rapid succession.

Unlike most peaks, a few curious events occurred. The amount of money people were making relative to how much they were spending was incredibly high. High levels of discretionary income translate to high levels of discretionary spending, which is what occurred in the late 1990s.

As a result of many factors, however, inflation was not running rampant, in part because of increased worker productivity made possible by improved technological efficiencies. Regardless, the lack of inflation led some people to believe that the economic expansion could and would continue forever. Nevertheless, interest rates were climbing higher, and eventually short-term rates exceeded long-term rates. This meant you could get a better interest rate if you locked up your money (based on maturity dates) only for one year than you could if you locked it up for ten years. Conventional wisdom states that the longer you must give up access to your money, the better the rate you should receive. Obviously, something had to give. (See Figure 5.8.) It's a dangerous time when the yield curve is inverted like this. You would think investors would have awakened and smelled the coffee by then. But they just kept dreaming.

RULE When the yield curve is inverted, we are in serious danger of a peak in the business cycle.

Optimism is eternal. We want to believe that the cycle will expand forever. When it comes to investing, many people will say, "Well, I will wait until things slow down before I sell." But when it does slow, they say, "Great; this is a buying opportunity."

FIGURE 5.8 The Inverted Yield Curve: Short-Term Interest Rates Exceed Long-Term Rates

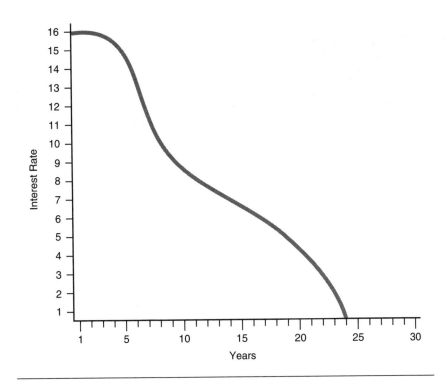

Ken Stern's School of Common Sense says:

- When your hairdresser buys a Mercedes as a result of his or her stock market gains;
- When you read stories that doctors are quitting their practices to become domestic helpers (butlers) because the pay is better;
- When you can't even get invited to a wine auction; and
- When start-up companies are buying multi-million-dollar ads for the Super Bowl;

We are peaking. Period. End of story.

Stage Four: Contraction

Characteristic signs of a contraction include these:

- A steep rate of decrease in projected earnings is seen.
- Inventories build up.
- Layoffs are typical.
- Interest rates start dropping (sometimes not the case, as in 1973–1974).
- Recession often follows.

Late in the expansionary phase, everything is going great guns. Companies are hiring, expanding, and growing fast just to keep up with demand.

Many factors can slow this demand: if a company overproduced, an increase in inventory could ensue. Profits could be squeezed as higher interest rates and higher wages affect a company's margins, which will ultimately lead to decreased business investment. Simply the thought of a slowdown can cause optimism to drop and prompt people and companies to become more conservative, which can slow the rate of economic growth. Even an unforeseen event, such as a war, can cause a short-term panic. Regardless of why, the one truth is that when the economy peaks, it usually peaks quickly and unexpectedly (unless you are paying attention to the business cycle), leaving most businesses and people vulnerable to financial shocks.

Immediately prior to the contraction, companies (and analysts following companies) were probably predicting record earnings and sales. So when the contraction begins, you will see companies miss these estimates. If a company expected 15 percent growth, and the economy slows, the company may only grow at 5 percent. Five percent growth, in and of itself, may not be terrible, but it is less than half of what was expected—which *is* terrible! Further, the company's stock may have been trading at a lofty level in anticipation of 15 percent growth. If the contraction continues and you are sitting on inventory you can't sell, if orders are canceled and a price war occurs, then even 5 percent growth may turn into zero or even negative growth. Ugh!

If something doesn't happen fast (see the next chapter), the economy could spiral into recession.

SUMMARY

Now you have the treasure map. You truly understand (probably as well as most economists) our economy. Sure, economists talk smart, raising questions about abstract theories such as supply-side versus demand-driven economies. They will passionately debate Keynesian ideas. It's abstract and academic. Focus on the issue at hand: how the business cycle makes you a better investor.

Accept the business cycle as a constant. If you trust the indicators and stick with your perception of what stage of the economy we are in, you will undoubtedly have an edge when deciding where and when to invest, as well as what sectors to favor.

CHAPTER SIX

Determining What Stage
of the Cycle We Are In

The grid of economic indicators on the next few pages will help you determine what phase of the economy we are in.

I suggest building or downloading these charts and graphs from the Internet. Meaningful trends are almost never visible on graphs with less than one quarter's data. This means that you can guess, but not decide, what stage of the economy we are in based on one month's data. Factors such as weather, a huge worker strike, or a few extra shopping days in a month can skew monthly data.

Even though the graphs and data tell a large part of the story, you must dig a bit deeper to determine accurately which phase we are in. For example, a graph of the manufacturing sector is not necessarily going to reveal if supply shortages exist.

At the peak of the economy, inflation was very tame—yet we still peaked. Not all of the indicators are going to move in lockstep. The rule is that when the majority of indicators move in a certain direction long enough to create a trend, you'll be able to better label the current phase.

INDICATORS OF THE CURRENT PHASE
OF THE BUSINESS CYCLE

Certain indicators, known as leading indicators, supposedly reveal what will happen next in the economy. Historically, the business cycle

FIGURE 6.1   Determining Where We Are in the Business Cycle

	Trough	Trough Early Expansion	Late Expansion	Peak	Early Contraction	Late-Stage Contraction
CONSUMER SENTIMENT						
Jumping Higher			✓	✓		
Gapping Lower					✓	
High Plateau				✓		
STOCK MARKET						
Starts to Decline				✓	✓	
Moving Sideways	✓					✓
Gapping Higher	✓				✓	
INFLATION						
CPI Gapping Higher			✓	✓		
PEAK						
PPI Gapping Higher				✓		✓
MANUFACTURING						
NAPM* Gapping Higher		✓	✓			
NAPM* Gapping Down					✓	✓
NAPM* Plateaus				✓		
Durable Goods Plateaus				✓		
CONSUMER DEBT						
Gapping Higher		✓	✓			
INDUSTRIAL PRODUCTION						
Capital Goods Orders Increasing Rapidly		✓	✓			
Capacity Utilization Extremely Efficient		✓				
INVESTMENT SPENDING						
Factory Orders Gapping Higher		✓		✓		
Factory Orders Gapping Lower						✓
INVENTORY						
Buildup				✓		
Dramatic Buildup					✓	✓

(continued)

FIGURE 6.1   Determining Where We Are in the Business Cycle, *continued*

	Trough	Trough Early Expansion	Late Expansion	Peak	Early Contraction	Late-Stage Contraction
CONSTRUCTION SPENDING						
Slows			✓	✓		
HOUSING STARTS						
Begin to Slow			✓	✓		
ECONOMIC GROWTH						
Real GDP Gaps Higher		✓	✓			
The Magazine Effect— Happy			✓	✓		
CONSUMER SPENDING						
Retail Sales Gap Higher		✓	✓			
Slow Growth In Retail	✓	✓				
INTEREST RATES						
No Change		✓				
Modest Increase			✓			
Aggressive Increase			✓	✓		
Aggressive Drop					✓	✓
THE YIELD CURVE						
Steep	✓	✓				
Normal		✓	✓			
Inverted			✓	✓		

*National Association of Purchasing Managers

has usually lasted about two and one-half years, but during the 1990s we experienced an extended period of expansion. In the meantime, how do economists determine where we are in the business cycle and why can't they pinpoint exactly where we are? Leading indicators, coincidental indicators, and lagging indicators—published by The Conference Board—show us where we are in the cycle. Leading indicators are easy to identify and generally signal a coming shift in the economy, so they can be used to predict an impending shift. Coincidental indicators are measures of the current economy. Lagging indicators are, as the name implies, indicators that confirm what phase we are in, but only after the fact. So we can't get a true picture until we can look at the lagging indicators along with the other indicators.

As a general rule of thumb, an impending recession is signaled by a decline in the Index of Leading Indicators for three consecutive months.

Leading, Lagging and Coincidental Indicators

Examples of these indicators are presented in the following sections.

Leading Indicators

Average weekly initial claims for unemployment insurance. New claims are an indication of increased layoffs. A decrease in the number of new claims is an indication that layoffs are occurring on a more infrequent basis. Therefore, new claims are a more sensitive factor in predicting a shift in the economy.

Although I agree that unemployment is a leading indicator, many factors would have occurred that would already have hinted that higher unemployment rates were imminent. A private outplacement firm, Challenger Gray & Christmas, actually tracks announced layoffs—an even earlier leading indicator.

Manufacturers' new orders of consumer goods and materials. Manufacturers take stock of their existing inventory and then place orders for materials needed to fill orders of consumer goods. Naturally, manufacturers use existing inventory before ordering new materials. Therefore, looking at manufacturers' orders is a more insightful early indication of change in the economy than actual consumer goods' orders.

Stock prices. Changes in the S&P 500 index reflect investor sentiment and the effect of interest rates on stock prices. Both investor sentiment and interest rates are good indicators of changes in the economy.

Money supply. The leading indicator is the inflation-adjusted figure of M2. When M2 does not keep pace with inflation, bank lending may fall. That is, when real money is not keeping up with inflation, banks will be less inclined to lend money. For the economy to grow, however, banks have to lend money.

Consumer expectations. The University of Michigan's Survey Research Center conducts a survey that asks for positive, negative, or unchanged responses in consumers' expectations of economic prospects for the family over the next 12 months, economic prospects for the nation over the next 12 months, and economic prospects for the nation over the next 5 years. If your expectations for the economy are not positive, don't you have a tendency to curtail spending? Most of us do, which is why this survey is a leading indicator.

Coincident Indicators

Personal income less transfer payments. Transfer payments is existing money that is moved from one source to another, such as Social Security payments. This figure includes all salaries and other income received, minus transfer payments. Income levels affect consumer spending and reflect the overall health of the economy.

Industrial production. Historically, changes in total output of the economy have been reflected in the physical output of all stages of production in the manufacturing, mining, and gas and electric utility industries on a value-added basis.

W*hat Is Money?*
- *M1 is currency in circulation plus demand deposits plus other checkable deposits.*
- *M2 is M1 plus money market deposit accounts plus savings and small time deposits plus balances of money funds plus overnight repurchase agreements at banks.*
- *M3 is M2 plus large time deposits plus term repurchase agreements at banks and savings and loans.*
- *L is M3 plus other liquid assets such as term eurodollars held by non-bank U.S. residents, bankers acceptances, commercial paper, Treasury bills, and other liquid government securities plus U.S. savings bonds.*

Manufacturing and trade sales. This aggregate level of spending on sales for manufacturing, wholesale, and retail businesses moves with the business cycle.

Lagging Indicators

Average duration of unemployment, average prime rate, commercial and industrial loans outstanding, and change in the CPI (consumer price index) for services are all lagging indicators.

EXPLANATION OF ECONOMIC INDICATORS

Gross Domestic Product (GDP)

This is probably the most widely followed economic measure. Quite simply, *the output of the GDP is the business cycle.* This measure is released quarterly, so everyone is anxious for the reading. The Bureau of Economic Statistics publishes the GDP, which is available online at <www.bea.doc.gov>.

Notice the GDP graph in Figure 6.2, whose data began in 1998. Let's assume that you didn't have the benefit of knowing the last spike down; a dramatic spike up would be an argument for a peaking economy.

You see that the graph ends after the first quarter of 2001. The end of the graph doesn't indicate a stabilizing trend, which means we had not yet hit the trough. The contraction phase was continuing. At that point, you should begin to look at more regular GDP data (monthly and especially quarterly) in an effort to determine when stabilization was occurring.

After the dramatic contraction in the GDP, it looked as though the peak was removed and the GDP was back to a normal level of growth. The concern is that we will go into a recession (i.e., negative economic growth). If that were the case, then there would be more to go on the downside.

National Association of Purchasing Managers Index

From this index, which can be found at <www.napm.org>, it appears as though companies went on a buyers' strike. Because consumer confidence was so low, companies all said at the same time, "Forget it." Factory orders looked as low as they did in 1991 (the last recession). I would have to say this is late-stage contraction, possibly a trough.

FIGURE 6.2   Gross Domestic Product

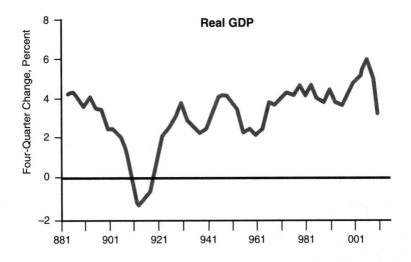

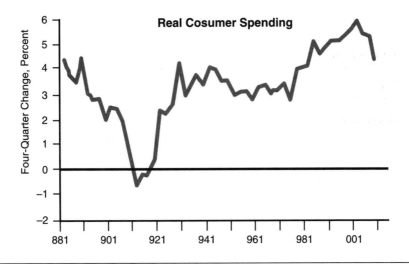

Also, look at the graph in Figure 6.2 during 1990 and 1991. What do you see? A dramatic decline followed by a dramatic uptick. This information is critical. First, the sudden downturn followed by an uptick illustrates what is known as a "V" formation. You may recall that the stock market performed terribly in 1990—before the GDP gapped down. The stock market performed well during 1991 at about the time the GDP was at its bottom. Unfortunately, many investors were not invested in 1991. The prevailing feeling at the time was that the economy was in terrible shape and stocks were doing poorly. As I will continue to repeat, Wall Street is a leading indicator and will anticipate changes in the business cycle. As a smart investor, you must read your economic indicators to determine where the economy will be six months from now, not where it was six months ago.

Factory Orders

The same thing is occurring with factory orders as with the National Association of Purchasing Managers Index. The figure for factory orders can be found at <www.stls.frb.org>.

Consumer Confidence

The University of Michigan tracks consumer confidence (see Figure 6.3), which tends to be a leading indicator and can be found at

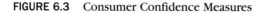

FIGURE 6.3   Consumer Confidence Measures

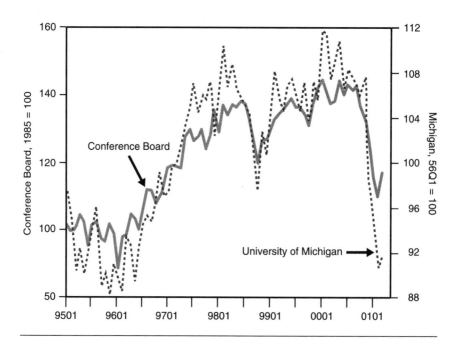

<www.conference-board.org>. Two factors can move an economy into or out of a recession; either consumers have to start spending money or corporations do. Usually it's consumers who lead the spending. If confidence is up, it's hoped that spending follows.

In Figure 6.2, the GDP was in a free fall. In Figure 6.3, we see that consumer confidence was as well. However, it looks as though a trend is developing that suggests confidence among consumers is stabilizing. I would now say this indication can be read as neutral. In addition, if the trend continues, it may signify a late-stage contraction to possibly a trough.

Construction Spending

Construction spending is a very good indicator, and it is not in a free fall. It didn't drop enough to signal a trough nor was it trending up. What's curious about this indicator is that construction spending is often a leading indicator of contraction. As inflation heats up, interest rates rise and construction spending slows. Clearly, after the first quarter of 2001, the economy is contracting, but construction thus far has not. I would say this indicator reads neutral but is to be watched closely. What would weigh heavily in favor of a recession is construction teetering on the fence or falling off. Housing starts, which measure new residential construction, are published once a month and are available at <www.census.gov/pub/const/www/c20index.html>.

Unemployment Insurance Claims

Although unemployment insurance claims are accepted as a leading indicator, announced layoffs are an even better leading indicator because when people are laid off, they typically curtail their spending. The fact that laid-off workers stopped spending money won't show up on a retail report, for example, until a month or two later. The figure for initial claims for unemployment insurance comes out once a week and is available at <www.dol.gov/dol/public/media/main.html>.

Consumer Price Index (CPI)

The CPI is a basket of goods created to measure pricing pressures on consumers. This figure is released monthly and can be found at <http://stats.bls.gov/news.release/cip.toc.html>.

The Magazine Effect

I count all the headlines that state the world is coming to an end. These colorful headlines are in fact scary enough to cause a depression. Before I sat down to write this chapter, I collected all the magazines and newspapers I had recently received. I counted 15, yes 15, different headlines talking about the end of the world.

This is a contrarian indicator, which is now giving a positive signal. When the crowd believes one thing, the opposite often occurs. The same is true if many headlines suggest the bull market has room to grow. Used as a contrarian indicator, current headlines are absolutely suggesting a trough.

SUMMARY

Think back to the beginning of year 2000. Look at the graphs I highlighted. In hindsight it was clear our economy was peaking. Everything from consumer confidence to manufacturing output spiked. Stocks reached ridiculous valuations. Forget academic arguments; common sense dictates that if we expand too fast for too long, something has to give. There comes a point that we don't want to, or can't, consume as much product. We need to digest, or simply burp an air bubble. If we really ate too much, we'll have to lie down and be sick for a while. Digesting and burping would indicate a contraction. Lying down sick would mean a recession.

Even if we agree that it would have been exceedingly difficult to predict the severity of an impending contraction, we could still have rationally asserted that a peak was close. What I just showed you is incredibly valuable information.

We can now discuss the government's involvement in our economy; like it or not, the government tinkers with our economy. Watch its moves and you'll be one step ahead of the game.

Smart Investments

PART THREE

Anywhere, Anytime

CHAPTER SEVEN

When in Doubt, Hedge Your Bets

"Ideas are a dime a dozen. People who put them into action are priceless."

Let's start with this first and most important rule:

RULE Regardless of the phase of the business cycle we're in or whether the market is racing ahead or dropping like a rock, there will always be investments that are rising and others that are falling.

As we have all unfortunately witnessed first hand, it is impossible to know what will cause the economy, or the stock market to move dramatically in the short-term. Who would have dreamed that terrorists would commit such unspeakable acts against the American people and the World Trade Center—just when the economy was picking up! Investors are foolish to react immediately to unexpected market phenomena. Even as such events help shape economic direction, an astute investor can find excellent investment potential amidst the rubble.

You want to capture as many of the rising investments as you can during all phases.

The business cycle provides the answers. Once investors learn how to read the business cycle, they see that it possesses one of the most important ingredients to making incredible investments in any market environment.

What is an investment sector? Just another way of talking about different areas of the market! Emerging markets, such as Third World countries, are one sector. Technology stocks are another sector. It's uncommon for all the available money to chase every area of the market at the same time; sometimes it's techs, sometimes health care, and sometimes utilities that are moving up.

Astute investors realize that patterns manifest themselves during each phase of the business cycle. Each is a little different, but that keeps it interesting and makes certain that you continue to do your research and respond accordingly. Historically, each market cycle has favored specific investment sectors. An investor's challenge is deciding what stage of a cycle we are in. Throughout this chapter you will learn key strategies to help you decide just that. It may seem odd placing weight on a sector rather than on a stock in deciding where to invest, but I assure you that getting the sector right is extremely important.

Although it's odd making investments based on a sector and not a stock, I assure you this is a very intelligent method to use when investing.

Did you ever play tag? Remember that you're "it" with the objective of touching someone else to be "it." Being "it" requires you to constantly run around trying to nab a person. However, you don't know what your opponent is thinking and your opponent has a vast number of directions in which to run. As a result, you are constantly running to where your opponents were, only to find them gone. If you begin to study your opponents, learn their movements, and act quickly, you should be able to anticipate your opponents' actions and reactions and tag one of them faster.

Investing is like tag; many investors constantly lose money, regardless of the direction of the market. I'll tell you why, but don't laugh even though it's so simple:

"Investors react to events that have already occurred instead of anticipating what is to come."

If you try to tag where a person *was,* you are going to wear yourself out. Stocks tend to follow macro-economic trends in the business cycle, so if you harness and understand the business cycle, you can anticipate the future movement of stocks.

If you only read the newspapers and analyze on stocks that performed the best recently, chances are you're looking at yesterday's news. As a result, you're going to spend a great deal of money and take on more risk than necessary.

RULE The stock market is a leading indicator of the economic cycle.

Good examples of this are sectors such as utilities and health care. These sectors tend to rise in anticipation that either the market has peaked or the economy is about to contract. Both can often happen well before the actual event occurs.

If an economist publicly states, "We are in a recession," take my word for it: the stock market has already dropped and is probably already in a bear market.

Consider the graph in Figure 7.1. Look at how stocks tend to trend lower before the peak in the economic/business cycle yet rebound and begin moving higher prior to the end of the slowdown (reces-

FIGURE 7.1   Economic/Stock Price Cycle

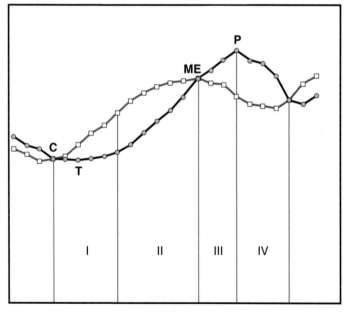

sion, or whatever you want to call it). Investors *anticipate* what is going to happen.

RULE Being in the right sector during each economic cycle is more important then being in the right stock.

As much as 94 percent of the return an investor receives is the result of being in the right sector.

When discussions about investing arise, people love talking about individual stocks. "Buy Compaq!" "IBM is the best!" "Ford Motor has a great new product." These are typical statements that I hear justifying why a certain stock should be bought. But what about buying the sector?

Study after study shows that if the sector is hot, chances are a particular stock in that sector will move higher—a rising tide raises all ships.

Consider the graph in Figure 7.2, which suggests that as much as 94 percent of the return an investor receives is the result of being in the right sector.

FIGURE 7.2   The Sector Is More Important Than the Stock

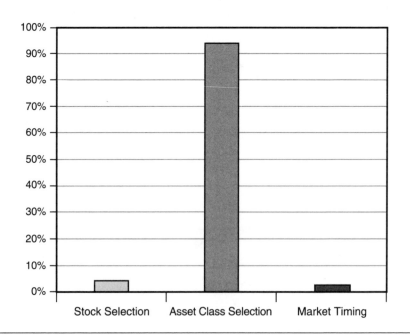

Don't get me wrong. I believe in owning and researching individual stocks, and I believe that an investor can find a stock that will outperform the sector. However, should you choose to never buy an individual stock again, I believe it would be possible to outperform the market simply by investing in the right sector at the right time.

The economic rotation will present opportunities for investors to rotate their sector weighting as the business cycle shifts. During each phase of the business cycle, certain sectors have traditionally outperformed other sectors. Using history as a guide but with further prudent research to decide where we are in the current cycle, investors can overweight the sectors they feel will benefit most.

▬▬
RULE Hedge your bets.

Face the fact that you won't be right about the direction of the economy every time. You will also not invest in every single one of the correct sectors or stocks 100 percent of the time. You must accept the fact that you will have some losses. Attempting to buy only winning sectors will increase your risk and the chance that you'll miss a surprise sector.

The best investors accept these facts and hedge their bets accordingly. They buy more of the sectors and stocks that they are most confident in, and they invest smaller amounts in the sectors where their confidence is low.

WHERE TO INVEST WHEN YOU ARE NOT SURE IF WE ARE IN A SLOWDOWN OR A RECESSION— AND YOU WILL NEVER BE SURE

It's February 15, 2000. The stock market just finished one of its best years ever. Everything is going gangbusters, not a cloud in the sky, and you're thinking about early retirement . . . maybe a Mercedes. Hey, you deserve it!

Hold on there, big fellow! Before you tell your boss to take a hike, let's go back to the business cycle. Use the grid in Chapter 6. What do you see? I see (and saw):

- Supply shortages
- Several interest rate hikes
- An inverted yield curve caused by a series of interest rate hikes

- Stocks trading at extremely high valuations (compared with historic values)
- Consumer confidence and other economic factors reaching all-time highs
- Historically low unemployment

What does this quick assessment suggest? It suggests caution and danger signals. It's true that no major inflation existed; it's true that many arguments could be made why the economy had legs to run. But there were enough signs to suggest that this was a time of caution— that the peak could be near.

Based on all of this, the following is what prudent investors should do:

- Overweight cash
- Overweight utilities, health care, food, beverages and tobacco (historically quality stocks)
- Increase bond holdings
- Sell capital goods stocks and industrial stocks
- Be ready to sell stocks that are vulnerable
- Make a list of "dream team" growth stocks that you would love to own

I use the term *overweight* to mean increase the percentage of your portfolio in that investment or sector. If you have had 10 percent in utilities, double the weighting to 20 percent.

This is what I did throughout the first and second quarters of 2001. Reading this, you have the advantage of not listening to experts talk about why the United States (or global economies) would or would not go into a recession or why stocks were cheap or expensive. Quite frankly, those opinions are not what mattered most. Follow your discipline and follow the facts. I make it sound easier than it is. When the markets are jumping 10 percent in a day, selling is hard to do.

Overweight Cash

Holding cash is a defensive play. When you aren't sure what is going on, it's smart to raise cash. It will provide you with funds should you wish to make future investments if and when the markets drop. Raising cash by selling investments can reduce your losses on these investments should the markets start going down.

As the market becomes more and more out of whack, you ulti-mately would like cash to represent 25 percent of your portfolio.

Overweight Utilities, Health Care, Beverages, and Tobacco

It's actually very logical. We need lights and medical services; and people eat, drink, and smoke. Stocks in these sectors may be inexpen-sive during the growth phase of the econ-omy simply because investors are looking for growth stocks that have the potential of yielding a higher return than stocks in de-fensive sectors. However, as the expansion matures, you will see an increased interest in defensive stocks. Don't forget, stocks will slip at the peak of the business cycle.

As stocks peak and begin to contract, defensive sectors traditionally outperform. Your portfolio might consist of 60 percent equities during this period. Of your equity weighting, you may want over half allocated to these defensive plays.

> **S**ocially Responsible Investing. *Over the last decade, more and more investors are refusing to invest in stocks that support industries inves-tors consider morally objectionable, such as tobacco. If you don't want to support, or benefit from, stocks such as these, just increase your holdings in other defensive sectors.*

Overweight Bonds

Bonds are another logical investment. If interest rates have increased during the expansion, the yield on bonds should be fairly attractive. Further, if the economy does begin to contract, interest rates may start trending lower. The effect is a good interest rate on bonds, and bonds may even appreciate in value as rates drop. If you bought a bond when it was yielding 8 percent and rates drop so current bonds are yielding 6 percent, investors will pay a premium for your 8 percent bond.

Sell All Capital Goods Stocks and Industrial Stocks

Machinery, manufacturing, and office equipment: stocks of com-panies producing these capital goods are probably having a terrific time. During a mature expansion, everyone needs the goods and ser-vices these companies provide. However, when the markets begin to drop, this will be the first category where spending cuts are made, so these stocks are very vulnerable during this stage of the cycle.

Be Ready to Sell Stocks That Are Vulnerable

I would not recommend selling a stock just to sell it or simply because you can realize a profit by selling it. You sell a stock when it is either grossly overvalued or is the wrong stock for the coming economic environment.

Sell Stop Orders—a strategy used to protect an investor from a stock falling below its support level. The broker-dealer holds the order, unfilled, until the stock hits the price the investor specifies. Then it is automatically sold.

When mania strikes, as it usually does in the stock market, stocks become overpriced. So take advantage of the stupidity of Wall Street; be a hero and get out before Wall Street realizes the error of its ways and tears the stock apart (i.e., feverishly selling it).

We don't know how high a stock will go and we don't know exactly when the economy will turn. Consider selling using *systematic sells* and *sell stop orders.*

Systematic Sells

Identify the stocks you own that are overvalued. Decide to liquidate your position in these stocks over the next two months. Sell the same amount of shares on a preset schedule, regardless of how the stocks are performing on that day. For example, decide to sell 200 shares every other Monday until you sell your total position of 800 shares.

Sell Stop Orders

Sell stop orders can also be used as protection on the downside. Often, you look at a chart and see that a stock will go down to a certain level but not below that level, which is called a support level. If the stock did break under this level, it could go as low as its next low. You may benefit by placing a sell stop order at just under the stock's last support. If the stock goes below the level, you are automatically sold out. If the stock continues to rise, you enjoy the additional appreciation.

Make a List of Dream Stocks

During the growth phase you'll miss certain stocks because you don't wish to purchase these companies at ridiculously high valuations. It doesn't mean you believe any less in the company. In fact, you may love the company's products or services, its management, or its consistency in hitting its earnings or revenue goals.

Still, make a list of these stocks. I don't suggest buying them if they have fallen in price. You'll want to see if they become undervalued; you'll also want to see if they lose earnings during a slowing economy. Perhaps you will never be able to buy these stocks—they may never attain a value acceptable to you. But then again, maybe they will.

As the economy slowed, I identified what I thought were some of the greatest companies in the world. My list contained companies that produced what we need. I also included companies with excellent management, and companies that I thought would be essential to our lives over the next ten years.

I made a list and checked it twice. I determined what price I was willing to pay for each stock. Some I was able to buy, others I wasn't. Following is a partial list:

KEN'S DREAM TEAM

- Citigroup (C)
- American Express (AXP)
- General Electric (GE)
- Sun Microsystems (SUNW)
- AOL Time Warner (AOL)
- Johnson & Johnson (JNJ)
- Nokia (NOK)
- Wal-Mart (WMT)
- Southwest Airlines (LUV)
- Corning (GLW)
- Lowe's Companies (LOW)
- Tyco International (TYC)
- AES Corporation (AES)
- Pfizer (PFE)
- Fannie Mae (FNM)

Notice that there is no uniform sector or market cap theme represented by these stocks. Some of the companies are large, while others are midsized. Some are in the health care industry and others in financial services or technology.

This may seem to contradict the earlier point about the importance of investing in the right sector at the right time. In a way, it does. When I invest, I follow a few investment strategies—and stick to the discipline of each of these strategies. Being in the right sector is a sector rotation strategy. Another strategy is what I call *core holdings.* These are stocks that I want to own for a long, long time. These are companies that I feel will influence the world, and their stocks will, over the long term, outperform major indexes. Yet I don't want to overpay for these stocks. I wait until these stocks fall into my web before I buy them—yet they are always in my sight.

SUMMARY

There is absolutely no way, with 100 percent accuracy, of predicting a contraction or recession. You must act on the belief that over the long term you are making excellent acquisitions and are hedging your bets. If we do go into a recession, you will probably see a temporary negative return on your portfolio. Trying to avoid any losses or negativity in your portfolio is unwise because you run the risk of turning into a market timer. Very few of us are smart enough for that. If you try to time the market, chances are you'll miss unexpected up days but still not be able to avoid unforeseen corrections. For the most part, stay invested; just change the allocation weighting and types of investments.

> *There is absolutely no way, with 100 percent accuracy, of predicting a contraction or recession.*

If we don't go into a recession, you are in a very prudent and probably profitable position. Will you make as much as those who invested 100 percent in growth stocks? No, but you were much less exposed to risk. Stop worrying about the next guy—worry about your own portfolio!

"Stop worrying about the next guy—worry about your own portfolio!"

CHAPTER EIGHT

Using the Business Cycle
to Cash In

"I laughed at the Lorax, 'You poor stupid guy! You never can tell what some people will buy.' Business is Business! And business must grow, regardless of crummies in tummies you know." —*The Lorax,* Dr. Seuss

Throughout this book, I have spoken freely of sectors and industries. Even though you know what these words mean, let's make sure we're talking about the same things.

- *Sector:* A grouping of companies along macroeconomic lines. As an example, Ford is a stock within the automobile industry, which is part of the consumer cyclical sector. Building materials, home furnishings, and hardware (to name a few) are also part of the consumer cyclical sector.
- *Industry:* A subsection grouping of companies with similar product lines or product mixes.

Following is a historical presentation of how various sectors of the market perform during various economic cycles. Accept that some investors may have anticipated a certain economic cycle before you did. As a result, the stocks and sectors that look like the places to be during various cycles may have already gotten expensive. This chapter is not about valuing the market, sectors, or stocks; that is examined in subsequent chapters. And although I believe valuing what you are buying is important, I think being in the right place at the right time is more important.

THE CONTRACTION

It's late summer 2000. Interest rates are peaking, stocks are falling, unemployment is increasing, and the mood of consumers isn't great. You check your trusty business cycle matrix and determine we are in a contraction with the very real possibility of a coming recession.

Soon we will discuss in detail how much to overweight or underweight; I allocate compared with the Standard & Poor's 500 index. (If the index is weighted 15 percent in utilities, you would have more than 15 percent of your portfolio in utilities.) The amount of cash you hold will also be discussed under asset allocation strategy. Without the benefit of an asset allocation model, however, it is prudent to increase cash to 20 percent or 25 percent during an uncertain economic period.

I always believe that long-term investors should be exposed to equities, but trying to time the market is filled with pitfalls. Investing is hardest to do during a contraction. When the economy is booming, stocks tend to get overvalued but tend to get undervalued during a contraction. During the good times, most sectors do OK, but during a decline, most sectors perform poorly. The best advice during this phase is to proceed with caution. Slowly add to the areas you feel will outperform but do so sparingly.

Commonsense actions to take while the economy is contracting include the following:

- Increase cash.
- If you're aggressive, prudently sell short stocks in the most unfavorable sectors.
- Place stops on questionable stocks.
- Increase your bond exposure.
- Further overweight sectors you feel would outperform during a contraction (see the discussion on the following pages on utilities, health care, financial services, and retail). Tobacco, food, and beverages would also be sectors to overweight.

Basically, what you are now doing is aggressively following through with the changes you began to make as a result of advice in the previous chapter, which assumed you weren't sure if the economy would begin to contract. Luckily, you got the jump during the peak of the business cycle, and now you are following through. (For a further explanation of these ideas, go back to the previous chapter.)

The one new idea not presented previously is the idea of selling stocks short.

Selling a Stock Short

This is possibly the most aggressive investment you can make. Here, you are betting that a stock is going to drop. Shorting a stock is temporarily borrowing a stock you don't own to be able to sell it. You profit when the stock falls far enough to more than cover the marginal interest you are charged to borrow (assuming the stock pays no dividends). You could also bet on a stock falling by purchasing a put option. A put gives you the right to sell the stock at a fixed price, the strike price, over a definite period. If the stock falls, the put option stands to go up in price.

Sounds great if you are correct about the stock dropping. However, what if the stock goes up? You have to buy it back. You can fill the contract (cover your short position) by buying it back whenever you choose. But what if you don't buy it back and the stock keeps rising? You can see why this is such a risky transaction. If you simply buy a stock, the worst is that the stock drops to zero and you lose all your money. But if you bet a stock is going lower and it, in fact, goes higher, it could theoretically rise to infinity, making your risk also infinity.

Some short traders have a mandatory sell price. If the stock rises 20 percent, they sell no matter what, take their lumps, and get out.

Defensive Sectors: A Case for Utilities, Health Care, Financial Services, and Retail

Historically, after interest rates are cut three times, utility stocks outperform all other sectors as measured one year after the third rate cut (see Figure 8.1). This is true both when a recession occurs or a recession is averted. If this trend holds for future declines, it seems that utilities are a very good asset class to be exposed to.

Health care is one sector that everyone believes people need, and it consequently displays an incredible macrotrend. As baby boomers age, the need for additional health care should continue. Ken Stern's School of Common Sense calls this a megatrend. Regardless of what this sector has done during other economic cycles, as a result of the megatrend, any dips should be used to increase your position so you're always weighted slightly higher than is the Standard & Poor's 500.

Financial services, transportation, and retail stocks are a big risk (see Figure 8.2). If the economy doesn't go into a recession and expansion is resumed, you make out like a bandit in each of these sectors except retail. If we do go into a recession, banks, brokerage firms,

FIGURE 8.1   The Case for Utilities as a Defensive Play

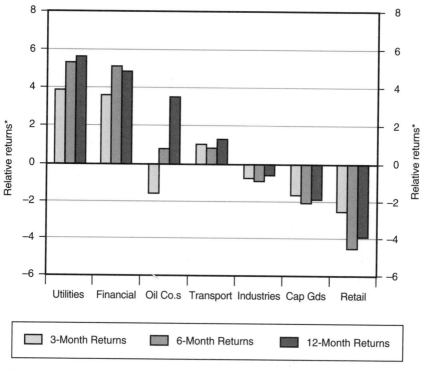

* Percent change from month of first easing relative to change in S&P 500.

credit card companies, and investment bankers continue to perform poorly—and so do their stocks. Consider Figure 8.3. What happened at the beginning of 2000 illustrates my point exactly. The real gross domestic product (GDP) started tanking and tanking fast. For about one month, all stocks were tanking (during periods of panic selling, there are very few places to hide). I became very excited during this period. Interest rates were going down, and, just as in every other downturn, it was simply a matter of time before certain sectors sprang to the forefront again. Notice how the GDP continued to spiral downward while the financial services index took off.

These are the trends that are fairly predictable and can be played when you understand the market cycle!

Retail is a slight enigma. It actually does better if we do go into a recession. The same rationale applies. Retail sales boom in stage one

FIGURE 8.2   Relative Returns for Various Sectors

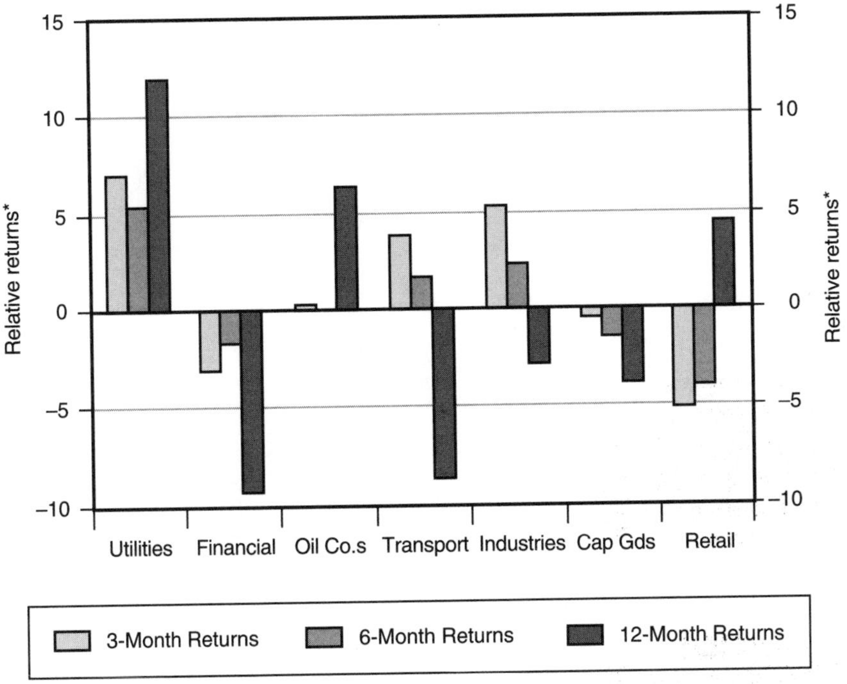

Legend:
- 3-Month Returns
- 6-Month Returns
- 12-Month Returns

* Percent change from month of first easing relative to change in S&P 500.

of an expansion. Investors know we will eventually emerge from a recession, so they get in early. But when an expansion does come, retail has traditionally performed poorly. This is a result of the fear of a slowdown. I would weight retail to 70 percent of the index.

The only other category that you should probably own when you're not sure if we will enter a recession is oil, which traditionally falls in the energy sector. Oil is somewhat volatile and is not discussed or emphasized nearly as much as it used to be, but some exposure makes sense during all cycles. I would always own oil stocks at a slight underweight to the market. In a later chapter, I explore energy, a sector I am very excited about. I do recommend portfolios overweight energy, but I think other stocks offer excellent growth potential other than oil fields.

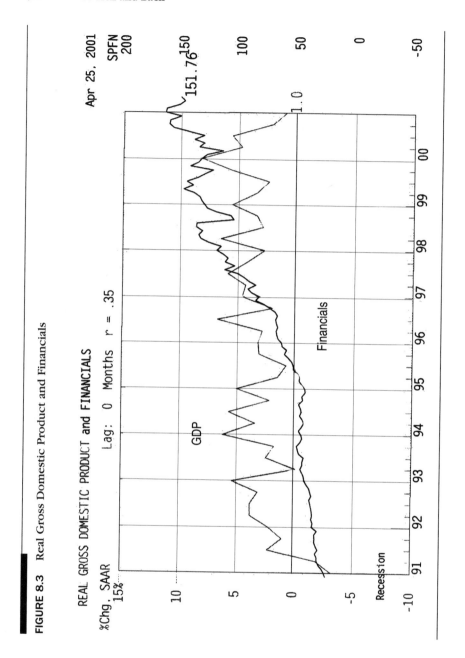

FIGURE 8.3   Real Gross Domestic Product and Financials

As you can see, there are no guarantees, which is why diversification makes so much sense. By being overweighted in certain sectors and underweighted in others, you hedge your bets. You won't make money on every investment, but at least you don't miss any of the sectors that experience growth.

What about Technology?

Technology, as a sector, has not been around long enough to get accurate data through many phases of the business cycle. That being said, it has been clear that certain areas of technology, such as semiconductors (which are chips), have proven to be a leading indicator during 2000, when the market was dropping, and in April 2001, when the market rebounded. We need more chips, memory, and speed to expand our computers as the market powers ahead. But as we saw, technology was one of the first areas to become overheated, experience supply shortages, and, ultimately, a loss in orders.

Based on how technology is beginning to behave, I would argue that, as a sector, technology will behave like a traditional growth stock. It will be the first to rebound from the trough and the first to peak.

THE SECTORS TO WATCH IF WE ARE ALREADY IN A RECESSION

At the risk of sounding repetitive (learning *is* repetition), if we are already in a recession, it's safe to say that stocks are already cheap. The next phase in the business cycle will be growth. As goods and services get cheaper, try and figure out where individuals and corporations will spend their money. If you can do this, you can more accurately predict which stocks to begin nibbling on.

If the economy is still gapping down and doesn't appear to have bottomed, stay defensive, as discussed previously.

However, begin to watch for signs that the bear market may be over, and get ready to be aggressive. It's almost time for offensive plays.

These simple statements are so easy to write, yet I understand how hard to do. At the end of September 2001, nobody could say for certain if the economy would have a prolonged recession, depression, or jump right back. We didn't know the extent of the war, and how it would affect the economy. So, it is better to stay defensive. But again, I am not reading the newspapers about yesterday and I am still buying stocks that I believe will be the best candidates for growth with the least amount of risk. After the terrorist attack, oil stocks dropped. They reached a point that I felt these stocks had a great deal of upside and little downside. So I bought. The multiples were cheap. The yield was good. If the economy slowed down too much, demand for oil would come down a little, and prices might come down as well. However, the increased use of the military would increase oil consumption. Further, the economy would rebound. And then the need for oil would be greatly enhanced. Who's to say for certain if I did the right thing? But I feel very fortunate to be able to buy oil and gas stocks as cheaply as I did.

Be Early to the Party

If we are in a recession, or the market has contracted, defensive stocks have probably already moved higher—even during a bear market. Most investors want to be defensive during a recession, but this is the time to begin making long-term investments.

In Figure 8.4, the performance of Anheuser–Busch (a classic beer stock) is compared with the Standard & Poor's 500 index. As you may recall, beginning in April 2000, the Nasdaq market began dropping and the S&P simply zigzagged until August and September, when it began dropping as well.

Almost the same day that the S&P began dropping, Anheuser starting climbing. This is classic. As investors became fearful of growth stocks, they reallocated (sector rotated) their funds into classic defense plays such as food, beverages, and beer.

The sector overheated and appreciated too fast. So in January 2001, when the market really looked bleak, Anheuser gave back most of its gains. This adds credence to my argument that you want to be early in getting into defensive stocks. You want to add to your defensive positions when the economy is peaking.

However, still considering Figure 8.4, when the S&P experienced a huge sell-off through February, Anheuser again took off. In fact, the entire beer, food, and beverage industry took off, as evidenced by the graph of Hershey Foods in Figure 8.5, which almost follows Anheuser's pattern identically. Defensive stocks shine during market sell-offs. In April, when it looked as though the S&P had started to climb again, the food stocks, including Hershey, sold off once more.

WHERE TO INVEST LATE IN THE TROUGH TO THE EARLY STAGES OF THE GROWTH CYCLE (BEFORE THE FIRST INTEREST RATE HIKE)

The period of time from trough to expansion is the filet for investing. It is the best part of the steak—tender and no fat to spit out. Stocks tend to rise the most during this period. However, most investors miss it because of two reasons: they are still shell-shocked from all the losses they just took and want to wait until the "market

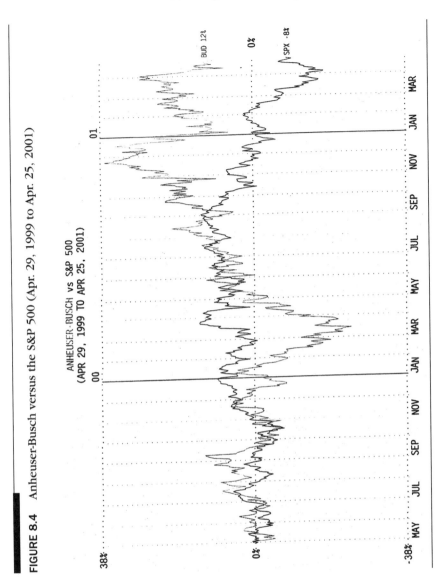

FIGURE 8.4   Anheuser-Busch versus the S&P 500 (Apr. 29, 1999 to Apr. 25, 2001)

starts to rise." The second reason is that the economy probably has not turned around yet. It is no longer gapping down, but unemployment could be at its peak and other negative indicators make it very difficult, psychologically, for investors to risk jumping back into the market. You can start buying during the recession, and I do. It will be a bit fatty and tough (meaning not every day is going to be up), but it's better to be early than miss the party. It's also important when beginning to invest aggressively to determine if any strong signals occur that the bear market is almost over. (See Chapter 10.)

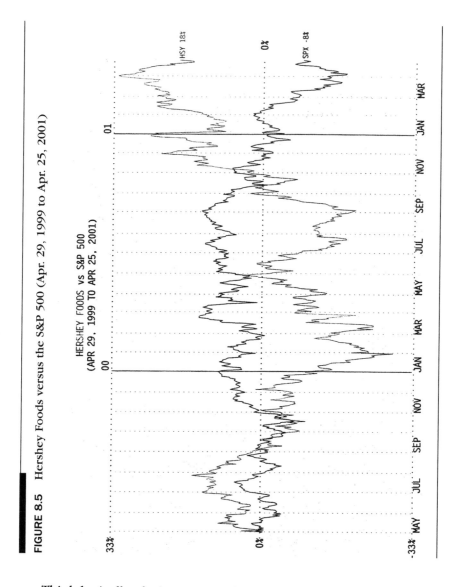

Think logically: during contractions or recessions, you and I stop buying homes and cars. We stop buying computers. Businesses don't purchase as many office supplies and don't overnight as many packages. As the economy grows, pent-up demand gathers steam. In fact, this demand has typically manifested itself at different times during the growth phase. Remember that every phase is different. Add your common sense to sector information along with the stock analysis skills you are about to possess from "Part IV: World-Class Stock Picking," and you will reach investor stardom.

Figures 8.6, 8.7, 8.8, and 8.9 list the sectors that historically do well during each phase of the business cycle, which doesn't mean that every cycle will be the same. The lists are meant as a guide and an illustration of trends.

WHICH SECTORS HISTORICALLY PERFORM THE BEST AND WORST AS GROWTH ACCELERATES?

Let's assume that the quick pop is over; earnings are still rising but not at the same feverish pitch. Interest rates have been bumped up once. Which sectors perform the best three months after the first rate increase?

FIGURE 8.6   The Best-Performing Sectors Historically at the Beginning of Growth

Autos	Trucking
Furniture	Technology
Broadcasting	Hotels and Leisure
Office Supplies	Gaming
Finance	

FIGURE 8.7   Best- and Worst-Peforming Sectors 3 Months after the First Interest Rate Hike

Best-Performing	**Worst-Performing**
Beverages	Metals
Personal Care	Aluminum
Truckers	Building materials
Computer systems	Lodging
Oil	Money center, Banks
Publishing	Heavy-Duty Trucks and Parts
Medical Products	
Containers (medical and glass)	
Auto Parts and Equipment	
Aerospace	
Utilities	

FIGURE 8.8   Best- and Worst-Performing Sectors 6 Months after the First
Interest Rate Hike

Best-Performing

Auto Parts
Beverages
Waste Management
Medical Products
Alcoholic Beverages
Computer Systems
Trucking
Restaurants
Oil
Broadcasting
Insurance
Steel
Airlines

Worst-Performing

Heavy-Duty Trucks and Parts
Building Materials
Gold and Other Precious Metals
Lodging
Home Building
Retail Stores

Six Months after the First Rate Hike

Notice now sectors such as oil and airlines are performing better. These companies usually have high relative fixed costs and are the second wave, if you will. The price of these goods firm after the economy is well into a growth stage. Notice, as rates rise, home building and building materials slow. Mortgages cost more, so people slow their buying pattern.

Twelve Months after the First Rate Hike

Now the economy is booming. But what's happening? People are worrying about a peak. The best sectors change dramatically to defensiveness yet again. People are selling oil, as this is a commodity that usually drops during a slowdown.

FIGURE 8.9   Best- and Worst-Performing Sectors 12 Months after the First
             Interest Rate Hike

Best-Performing	Worst-Performing
Health Care	Apparel
Beverages	Autos
Medical Products and Supplies	Building Materials
Broadcasting	Oil
Restaurants	Chemicals
Tobacco	Retail Stores
	Household Furniture
	Home Building

HOW TO FIND STOCKS WITHIN A SECTOR
AND WITHIN AN INDUSTRY

The previous discussion clearly illustrates how various sectors behaved and performed during different economic cycles. As investors, we need to find the stocks within each industry and within each sector. For assistance, see Figures 8.10 to 8.12.

Again, I want to reiterate that the best time to get in is *before* a recession.

SUMMARY

It has always amazed me how important being in the right sector at the right time is; yet very few investors speak of this. They speak of individual stocks.

The economy is tricky and difficult to predict with 100 percent accuracy. But once you get past this fact, it is reasonable to determine what phase of the business cycle we are in. Finding the right sector based on this information is a critical component to your overall investment strategy. Use it!

FIGURE 8.10   Examples of Sectors, Industries, and Stocks within an Industry

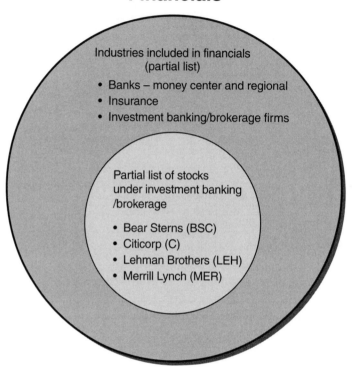

SECTOR:
Financials

Industries included in financials
(partial list)

- Banks – money center and regional
- Insurance
- Investment banking/brokerage firms

Partial list of stocks
under investment banking
/brokerage

- Bear Sterns (BSC)
- Citicorp (C)
- Lehman Brothers (LEH)
- Merrill Lynch (MER)

FIGURE 8.11   Examples of Sectors, Industries, and Stocks within an Industry

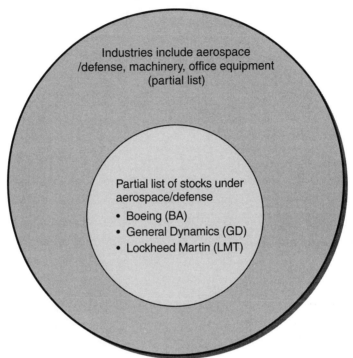

SECTOR:
Capital Goods

Industries include aerospace
/defense, machinery, office equipment
(partial list)

Partial list of stocks under
aerospace/defense

- Boeing (BA)
- General Dynamics (GD)
- Lockheed Martin (LMT)

FIGURE 8.12   Examples of Sectors, Industries, and Stocks within an Industry

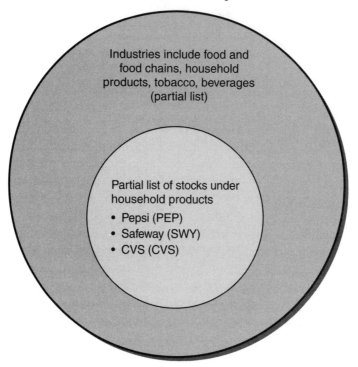

SECTOR:
Consumer Staples

Industries include food and
food chains, household
products, tobacco, beverages
(partial list)

Partial list of stocks under
household products
- Pepsi (PEP)
- Safeway (SWY)
- CVS (CVS)

CHAPTER NINE

The Easy Way
to Beat the S&P

Investors actively invest in an effort to achieve the highest returns possible with an acceptable risk. A strong debate exists whether an individual investor can actually actively invest and beat the returns of passive investing. Passive investing is simply placing your money in an index and letting it go. Much has been written on the returns of the popular benchmark, the Standard & Poor's 500 (S&P 500).

The S&P 500 is a grouping of 500 stocks that is used as a benchmark for a particular market. It consists of large companies that are meant to be a sample of the overall market. In fact, the size of the companies within this index represents about 70 percent of the total value of all stocks that trade on the New York Stock Exchange and the Nasdaq (the over-the-counter exchange).

Admittedly, the S&P 500 has outperformed many actively managed mutual funds and individual investors, but this doesn't mean it is impossible to beat the S&P 500. In fact, I believe two strategies could clearly enable an investor to beat this index. In this chapter I explore macroeconomic trends to identify areas of growth that may enable an investor to beat the market. In the next chapter, I'll discuss a method for beating the S&P without buying individual stocks.

USING MACROTRENDS TO BEAT THE S&P 500

There are two broad methods of investing in stocks: the first is a top-down method and the second a bottom-up method. The *bottom-*

up method is a way of searching for stocks through a model of preset criteria of your choosing. (See Chapter 12.) The *top-down* method for investing is a strategy that explores certain macroeconomic trends. From this information, investors decide which sectors they wish to be most heavily invested in. Once these sectors are determined, the best stocks in each sector are defined.

Earlier, I stated that most of an investor's return is based on being in the right area of the market, not on individual stock selection as most investors wrongly believe. During periods when we could be in a recession or a bear market, top-down investing can be a terrific way to diversify and reduce risk by betting on a long-term trend.

As an active investor, my goal is to try to beat the returns of passive investments. The S&P 500 is passive because it doesn't regularly buy or sell the stocks in the index. A mutual fund is active because it is constantly buying and selling in an effort to beat the market.

In the previous chapter we used the business cycle to identify sectors that may be better for building a position. Other macroeconomic trends can be extremely valuable in providing investors hot clues necessary to identify areas that are ripe for expansion.

One popular macrotrend that I have been watching for a long time is health care. Baby boomers are aging, so the need for health care products and services is exploding and should continue to. Based on this macrotrend, I will probably overweight health care for the next several years.

Another way to consistently beat the S&P is to find the blockbuster sector, that is, the one with the hottest economic trend for a particular decade. Find the best stocks in that sector, and hang on! In the 1990s, the sector that received the most attention—and growth—in the Standard & Poor's 500 was technology and communications. This sector now makes up roughly 26 percent of the S&P 500.

> *Earlier I talked about overweighting your stock portfolio compared with other investments in your personal portfolio. For this chapter, overweight is to be interpreted as having a larger allocation compared with the S&P 500 index.*

Over the years, certain sectors will grow, causing those sectors to become a larger percentage weighting of the S&P 500. Two years ago, technology represented over 10 percent more of the index than it does now. A decade ago, oil was much more heavily weighted.

One of the ways to beat the index is to foresee which sector is going to be the next one or two to experience substantial growth. An investor who can foresee this may wish to overweight that sector. This is where you are going to have to be a true visionary. I greatly respect real estate visionaries who can look ahead a few years and establish a path of growth. These visionaries purchase real estate at dirt cheap prices in seemingly undesirable areas, which then become the next hottest growth areas.

In the same vein, outstanding investors can identify certain industries that should experience dramatic growth and expansion in the coming years. They will then use short-term business cycles and Wall Street stupidity to find an entry point for building their position. Following are two ideas I present to show you how to do the research. It is now up to you to find areas that you understand to build your own portfolio.

MULTICULTURALISM

Scanning the papers the other day (I was reading my local paper, not doing industry research), I came across a story that stated Caucasian people in California were now considered the minority. The influx of Asian and Mexican people tipped the tide, so to speak. The article continued to note that California was the third state, after Hawaii and New Mexico, in which Caucasians were a minority. Furthermore, based on census information and demographic trends, it was predicted that white Americans would continue to become more of a minority while Asians and Hispanics would continue to increase.

In fact, the rise of multiculturalism is probably the second biggest demographic trend behind the surge of baby boomers (another incredible macroeconomic trend that you should look at in your top-down analysis). As my wheels turned I thought, Wow, there must be a way to capitalize on this.

Let's first determine if multiculturalism is, in fact, a trend (not a fluke) and if it is big enough to make money from it. So start reading economic reports, read the newly released 2000 census, read *American Demographics.* I did, and what I found is illustrated in Figure 9.1

Non-Hispanic whites fell to 69 percent of the total U.S. population, down from 76 percent ten years ago, and appears to be a fairly substantial trend. Ten years ago, one in five Americans was considered a minority. Today, it's one in four.

So how do we make money from this? Do minorities have any special buying habits? What is their family structure like? If we can answer these questions, perhaps we can find opportunity.

In fact, one of the most visible market forecasters and technicians on Wall Street is Ralph Acampora. His popular book titled *The Fourth Mega Market* discusses multiculturalism. He states that the influx of

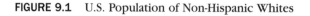

FIGURE 9.1   U.S. Population of Non-Hispanic Whites

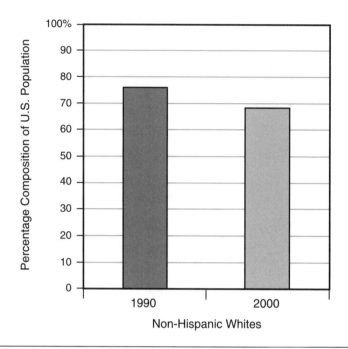

Europeans in the 1800s was a large factor in the bull market of 1877 to 1891.

Financial Services

I talked about the growing population of Hispanic people in the United States, whose population and wealth are both growing. Many need access to credit and financial services, including home loans and mortgages, bank loans, and credit cards.

Investors can search the financial services sector to find which companies provide financial services. Investors can go to their public library to search books such as Standard & Poor's research books or *The Value Line Investment Survey.* If you're interested in financial services, simply read about all the stocks in that sector. Study if their business plans include soliciting various segments of the population. If library research is not sufficient, go to companies' Web sites for further research. A company's annual statement may report geographic makeup of loans. If you're still not finding the information you need, call a company and ask to speak to shareholder services. That department should be able to answer your questions or point you in the right direction. One other excellent method of research is to call and ask a financial advisor to find a research report on a particular company or companies. A good advisor should have access to research reports from various analysts. It may also behoove an investor to look at institutions marketing to the Hispanic market.

I found three companies that lend money to the groups that I discussed. Figure 9.2 is an example of one that I decided to buy.

Household International was a "sleeper" that was not getting much attention. However, research showed it lent money primarily through credit cards. Its biggest customers included union workers, who tend to have lower default rates—important during economic slowdowns. As you'll learn when we study the fundamentals of a company, the fundamentals of this company seemed very strong and reasonably priced. Earnings and revenue were growing strongly; yet considering how much you were paying for this earnings and revenue growth (see "Key Ratios" in Figure 9.2), you weren't paying too much for the stock.

Household was a great stock that served us well. We did sell, and didn't get the highest price it ever reached. However, when the terrorist attacks occurred, we placed stops on many of the stocks we felt could be vulnerable to a earnings slowdown. We calculated which stocks would be historically overvalued because of slowing earnings and a higher stock price. Household hit that list. As we (the portfolio managers at Ken Stern & Associates) often do in uncertain cases, we placed a stop on the stock. When the stop level was reached, the stock was sold. It was a good run and time to move on. However, we will continue to watch this stock, and if it goes low enough, it may reappear on another value screen. Because I still feel strongly about macro-trends, I would be happy to have the chance to buy the stock back.

Broadcasting

Many larger media and broadcasting companies have begun to buy Hispanic radio stations. Do a search of your car radio: how many Hispanic stations do you hear when searching? How about on your home TV?

I researched all of this by searching the Standard & Poor's 500 index for broadcasting stocks. I read about each one and found one stock in particular that focused on the Spanish market, Univision. Some people may come to the same conclusion by simply watching the

FIGURE 9.2   Household International, Inc. (HI)

Household Int'l (HI)

2700 Sanders Road
Prospect Heights, IL 60070
(847) 564-5000 Investor Contact: Celeste Murphy
www.household.com

May 25, 2001 .... 66.27

Price Chg - YTD	20.5%
Dividend Yld	1.3%
P/E............................	18.

1,619,400

Capitalization	
% LT Debt to Total Cap	85%
Owned by Institutions	80.7%
Market Capitalization	31.2 Bil
Avg Daily Vol(Last 30 days)	1,881,330

Business Overview
Household International, Inc. provides consumers in the US, UK, and Canada with a variety of loan products. The company offers home equity loans, sub-prime automobile finance loans, MasterCard and Visa credit cards, private-label credit cards, tax refund anticipation loans, and other types of unsecured loans. Household International also offers credit and specialty insurance in the US, UK, and Canada. The company, which serves over 45 million customer accounts, operates 1,378 consumer finance branch offices in 46 US states, 85 branches in 10 Canadian provinces, and 176 branches in the UK.

			Growth Rates
Earnings	**$**	**%**	**5 Yr Historical**
Latest Quarter (Mar 01)	.91	up 17%	
Latest 12 Months	3.68	up 15%	20%
First Call Consensus			**LT Future**
Current Quarter (Jun 01)	.93	up 16%	
Year Ended Dec. 01	4.08	up 15%	15%
Year Ended Dec. 02	4.65	up 14%	
Revenues			**5 Yr Historical**
Latest Quarter (Dec 00)	3.3 Bil	up 27%	
Latest 12 Months	12 Bil	up 26%	18%
Dividends			**5 Yr Historical**
Indicated Rate & Yield	.88	1.3%	
Increases Last 5 Yrs	5		11%

Key Ratios & Measures	5 Year Range	Current
P/E	9 - 29	18
Price to Book	1.7 - 4.2	3.8
Price to Cash Flow	7 - 18.3	15.3
Price to Sales	1 - 3	2.61
Return on Equity	9.3% - 24.1%	24.1%

BETA S&P 500	1.27

station. When the company airs a station identification, simply call and ask if it is publicly traded or is owned by a publicly traded company.

Consider the graph of Univision in Figure 9.3. This is a company I was very interested in but decided not to buy. My associates and I thought it was in the right industry; and appealing to the Spanish

FIGURE 9.3   Univision Communications Inc.

Univision Comm (UVN)

1999 Avenue of the Stars,#3050
Los Angeles, CA 90067
(310) 556-7676
www.univision.net

Jun 07, 2001 46

Price Chg - YTD	12.4%
Dividend Yld	0%
P/E............................	104.5

Capitalization						
% LT Debt to Total Cap	32%					
Owned by Institutions	99.6%					
Market Capitalization	9.5 Bil					
Avg Daily Vol(Last 30 days)	940,765					

Business Overview

Univision Communications Inc. is a Spanish-language television broadcaster. The company's Univision Network provides 24-hour-per-day Spanish-language programming with a prime time schedule of substantially all first-run programming throughout the year. Univision owns and operates nearly 20 stations and has affiliation agreements with about an additional 30 TV stations and 1,100 cable affiliates. Univision also owns Galavision, a Spanish- language cable network that reaches about 3.6 million Hispanic subscribers. In addition, the company operates radio stations, owns advertising billboards, operates Univision.com and has joint ventures with Fingerhut and Ask Jeeves. In Dec 00, the company agreed to acquire USA Broadcasting.

			Growth Rates
Earnings	**$**	**%**	**5 Yr Historical**
Latest Quarter (Mar 01)	.03	dn 67%	
Latest 12 Months	.44	up 10%	NM
First Call Consensus			**LT Future**
Current Quarter (Jun 01)	.13	dn 7%	
Year Ended Dec. 01	.48	dn 4%	28%
Year Ended Dec. 02	.46	dn 4%	
Revenues			**5 Yr Historical**
Latest Quarter (Mar 01)	195 Mil	up 7%	
Latest 12 Months	877 Mil	up 19%	30%
Dividends			**5 Yr Historical**
Indicated Rate & Yield	NA	0%	
Increases Last 5 Yrs	NA		NA

Key Ratios & Measures	5 Year Range	Current
P/E	41 - 223	104.5
Price to Book	3.9 - 20.5	13.5
Price to Cash Flow	11.2 - 77.8	59.8
Price to Sales	2.9 - 15.2	10.83
Return on Equity	2.6% - 26.8%	14.2%

BETA S&P 500	0.68

broadcasting market fit our megatrend concept. However, the stock was simply too expensive for our taste.

Although revenue and earnings had been increasing, they did slow dramatically with the slowdown in the economy. The stock dropped as well but not enough. Trading at 100 times earnings, 13 times book value, 59 times cash flow, and 10 times sales makes it simply too expensive based on growth.

We will continue to watch and monitor this stock in hopes of one day owning it.

Global Trends

Investors may find it makes sense to heed global trends. One trend in particular is the use of power. Unless you have been living in a cave, you know the search for power has been nothing short of monumental. I live in California, and my electric bill is going through the roof. When I talk with friends in other countries, I find developed countries are facing similar energy problems, and nondeveloped countries seek more and more energy too.

Energy affects every aspect of our life. More and more people using computers, faxes, and printers sucks energy. Automobiles, ships, and airplanes suck energy. This trend is almost too big to truly grasp.

So the questions are: Will the need for energy continue? Is this already reflected in stock prices? What segments of power will be most lucrative for individual investors? Clearly energy can be considered an important trend. You must decide how to play it.

SUMMARY

Through the years, macroeconomic trends will develop. Regardless of whether the trend is toward faster computers, health care, or energy, it is safe to assume that there will always be trends.

I find investing in trends a fairly easy investing style. It's usually long term (more so than, say, sector rotation) and fairly easy to identify. In general, can we agree that people will need health care and health care related services in the future? Can we agree that as the population ages and mortality rates rise, the need will rise exponentially? Health care is a no-brainer. The difficulty is deciding if you want to be in biotech, pharmaceuticals, nursing homes, etc. That's why you need to read the sections on individual stock picking or simply buy the index. If you feel comfortable choosing the right trend, you now have the option of researching the best stocks to invest in within the trend you have identified. You may opt to find a sector mutual fund or specialty index fund (see the next chapter) that will make investments to match the macrotrend you've identified.

CHAPTER TEN

How to Spot
a Market Bottom—
Time to Get Aggressive

WHAT ARE THE SIGNS
THAT THE BEAR MAY BE OVER?

Stop reading newspapers for investment guidance. By the time you read about it in a newspaper, it's happened. Newspapers are paid to print yesterday's news. Investors forecast the future.

Even though it's important to identify bull and bear markets, it's not as important as identifying the current economic or business cycle. The subtitle of this book alludes to the fact that investors should be able to make savvy investments regardless of whether the market is bearish or bullish.

If you know we are headed toward a bear market as suggested perhaps by the economic cycle, it may be prudent to reallocate your portfolio and batten down the hatches. It was interesting to note, as I did in Chapter 6, that the stock market began falling before the growth phase was complete. Thus, stocks are a leading indicator. So if you were trying to find the stock market bottom, it would make sense to have a few indicators. There are many, and they tend to work well in helping you decide when you want to jump back in.

Before going into the explanation, I've created a handy grid for you to use to determine the end of the bear:

FIGURE 10.1   Determining the End of a Bear Market

Answering yes to the following questions indicates a strong possibility that the bear market is going into hibernation.

	YES	NO
MONETARY POLICY		
Is the Fed aggressively easing interest rates?	X	
Have rates been cut at least three times?	X	
Are signs of inflation easing?	X	
Is the yield curve inverted?		
DOWNSIDE LEADERSHIP		
Are large numbers of stocks reaching new lows?	X	
BONDS		
Are people buying bonds?	X	
Are more experts recommending buying more bonds?	X	
MAXIMUM EARNINGS DISAPPOINTMENTS		
Are companies missing their estimates?	X	
Are companies beginning to provide positive guidance?	X	
FORMAL RECESSION		
Is the economy in a formal recession?	X	
CONSUMER CONFIDENCE		
Is confidence in the economy low but stabilized?	X	
VALUATIONS		
Have stocks dropped below their historical values?	X	

A positive indicator means the bear market is almost over; a negative indicator means it isn't; neutral means neutral.

IF THE MARKET DROPPED BECAUSE OF
A RECESSION, WHAT WOULD IT TAKE
TO GET OUT OF A RECESSION?

It is extremely important to know what it takes to get out of a recession. I repeat this theme throughout the book: The best time to buy stocks is when the economy is still in horrible shape, when it looks the worst and is at a bottom (trough).

The concern among investors is when do we know we have bottomed out and how long will the bottom last? A recession could last three, even four, years. Boy, that's a long time to be sitting on your investments wondering if there will be money left when you need it. So it's prudent to have some visibility, some inkling when a recession or contraction will come to an end. Understand that if you wait until there are signs of life—the patient isn't dead—chances are we have already begun phase one of the expansion. Waiting and buying at this stage has probably diminished your risk, but stocks have already begun to rise. Because stocks are a leading indicator, they will move before the event occurs.

I believe you can look at several factors to decide if the cycle has bottomed out. Signs of an economic bottom include:

- Cheap stocks
- Stabilization of consumer confidence
- Falling interest rates to a stable yield curve
- A bottom in the housing market
- Fewer jobs being lost than in the previous few months
- Increases in consumer spending (Consumers usually spend our economy out of a recession.)
- Lower taxes

When the economy and stocks are expanding during the final period of an expansion phase, you'll begin to be concerned with the peak. During the contraction phase in the economy, you start looking for signs of capitulation. Think of capitulation as throwing in the towel. A large, dramatic, and negative event or a series of negative occurrences will take place: a dramatic sell-off in stocks, extremely large lay-off notices, a dramatic (not orderly) drop in various economic indicators such as manufacturing.

When these events occur, the market should be close to bottoming out. Stocks will be incredibly cheap, although most "experts" will state that stocks could go cheaper if the economy doesn't quickly recover from a recession. If you are asking yourself, What's a cheap stock? I applaud you. This is a very difficult question to answer and one I attempt to answer throughout the book (see "Part IV: World Class Stock Picking"). For purposes of this discussion, I am not concerned with timing or charts and technical research. I consider a stock cheap when I believe enough people consider the company cheap enough to be bought as an acquisition—that is, once a stock gets cheap enough, other companies simply buy the company out.

Ironically, in April 2001, when my group began aggressively buying stocks again, I didn't think stocks were cheap. Yet I still bought. I won't lie and tell you this didn't make me nervous. However, other strong factors and arguments helped us make the decision to prudently buy the stocks we were comfortable with, a topic I discuss later. Yet, because I thought many stocks were still expensive we purchased stocks cautiously. We invoked many stop orders on these stocks in case we were wrong. The markets softened a bit later in year 2001, and then in September we saw some of the worst stock market moves in history after the terrorist attacks. We repositioned the portfolio as if the economy were in a recession. Yet, we were also using bottom-up analysis, and buying growth stocks as well. We still felt the economy was close to bottom. Knowing that stocks would rebound before the economy, we slowly increased our exposure to stocks through the rest of year 2001. Although we were unsure, we followed our discipline. I previously outlined what factors would be necessary to get out of a recession. Many of the events that would need to occur were occurring: cheap stocks, low interest rates, lower taxes, etc. Again, I don't know how the most recent purchases will turn out in the short-term, but for the long-term I am feeling pretty lucky to have the opportunity to buy stocks when they are on sale.

It's a fair assumption that when stocks continue to hit new lows, consumer confidence has probably already dropped dramatically. Further drops in consumer confidence won't be as large and, in fact, confidence might begin to rise as cheap stocks are purchased.

Interest rates will be sitting at their lowest level in many years. Previously, the Federal Reserve might have aggressively lowered interest rates by 0.50 percent or maybe more. Rates dropping 0.25 percent or not at all could be a sign that the trough is almost over. The same is true regarding unemployment. After a big drop in unemployment, the next few weekly and monthly reports should stabilize if we are entering an expansion phase.

When either of these two scenarios occurs, it's time to get ready for serious turbulence. Until you have a little more information, such as when you are flying into a rainstorm but don't know if it's mild or a tornado, be conservative. Slow your speed (reduce risk) and observe.

Allocate your portfolio as you would during an economic peak. Throughout the chapter, "Using the Business Cycle to Cash In," the behavior of each sector of the market was studied. I determined that it was prudent to know that certain sectors in a bear market outperformed other sectors. When you believe that more than an average chance exists that a bear market is heading our way, (1) reallocate funds to overweight those sectors that may outperform the market, (2) raise cash, and (3) place stops on your vulnerable stocks.

Monetary Policy

When the Fed aggressively cuts interest rates three to four times, we are getting close to a bottom.

Downside Leadership

More stocks hitting new lows signals a bottom. *Investor's Business Daily* and *Barron's* have good measures of this to track. The *Barron's* graph in Figure 10.2 is a wonderful, yet easy, measure that can help an investor decide if the market may be heading in any one direction. Because the Dow Jones Industrial Average is made up of only 30 stocks, the Dow was down on many days when the overall market was up, as measured by the advance/decline (A/D) lines and breadth. If you consider all the stocks that trade on a given day (not just the Dow), and more stocks advance than decline, you have a positive advance/decline line. So, in fact, the A/D line could be higher even if the Dow is down. The stronger the A/D line, the better the breadth of the market.

Many investors watch the breadth of the market to see if it begins to form a trend in one direction. If it does, they believe that the Dow Jones Industrial Average will move accordingly. So in the example in Figure 10.2, notice how the breadth began moving higher beginning in December, while, simultaneously, the Dow was still plummeting. However, by April the Dow took off. The previous strong breadth in the market that preceded the Dow's rise indicated this was going to happen. Instead of catching a falling knife, it may be prudent to wait until the downside leadership has stabilized.

Also watch the advance/decline line, which shows the number of stocks that are moving higher compared to the number moving lower. When most stocks are moving lower, the A/D line is negative. I watch for a big blowout on the downside and then a pattern of stabilizing. A prudent investor always waits for a pattern. If you are see-

FIGURE 10.2 Watch the Advance/Decline Line for Clues

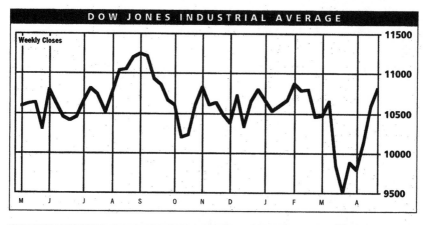

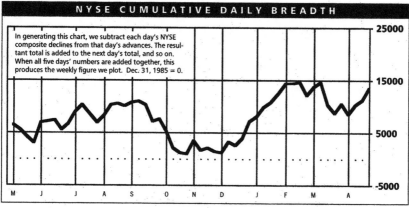

ing 80 or 90 new lows a day, wait until that trend begins to ease up a bit. You probably won't call the bottom (meaning the market might go up a bit), but at least you are not taking as much risk.

Bonds

Bonds tend to underperform stocks over time, although, like stocks, they are driven by supply and demand. When stocks look as though they are absolutely at their worst, investors flee to the safety of bonds, and the bond markets surge. If you think about it, it *is* kind of silly. If the Fed has cut rates several times in succession and you start buying bonds when interest rates are low, chances are the next cycle will be positive for the stock market, and the Fed will, at some point, have to stop easing interest rates and return to a neutral policy and probably, eventually, a tightening policy. If that is true, then chances are the bond market will decrease in value over time, which proves the existence of "the herd effect"—most investors doing the wrong thing at the wrong time. Nevertheless, when this scenario starts, you should start buying stocks.

Maximum Earnings Disappointments

All the analysts that track a stock make predictions about what they think the company will earn in a given quarter. Companies like First Call create a consensus that astute investors track. In April 2001, when companies reported earnings for their previous quarter, the number of earnings disappointments was incredibly high. Big companies saw, in many cases, earnings and revenues drop 70 to 80 percent. But three things happened, two of which are applicable here.

For the first time in almost a year, companies again began to provide guidance for future quarters. Companies hate to provide any guidance to analysts because the stock will probably be taken out behind the barn and shot (along with the management of the company) if they are wrong. But they know that any positive guidance will help the stock price and, they hope, the company. As the economy contracted, these companies had no visibility; they simply had no idea what they would earn over the next two quarters. But in April 2001, many companies did provide guidance, noting that the next quarter could be a bottom.

The second thing that happened was the price of a company's stock itself. In some cases, so much bad news was figured in that the stock was historically cheap. At some point investors think the stock is too cheap, and they begin to buy.

The third thing that happened was an unexpected .50 percent cut in interest rates by the Fed. This improved the mood of the market and set the tone for a recovery.

Many Web sites track earnings. Go to <www.msn.com>, click on earnings announcements, and then select First Call.

Formal Recession

I find the announcement of a formal recession a wonderful signal that the bear market is almost over. If there is enough evidence to state that our economy is in a recession, chances are we are closer than not to coming out of it. And because stocks are a leading indicator, they will move higher before the economy does.

Read newspapers or specific magazines such as *The Economist* to decide if we are in a formal recession.

Consumer Confidence

When I see a dramatic downward movement of consumer confidence, I safely assume the economy is contracting. I know it's consumers' spending that typically pulls the economy out of a recession.

When I see a pattern of consumer confidence stabilizing (albeit way down), it's a sign to me that the bear market is almost over.

Valuations

Regardless of the economy, when stocks get cheap enough, people begin to invest. You can track valuation of the market in two ways: through a technical graph pattern or through fundamentals. Let's do both.

The graph in Figure 10.3 represents the performance of the Standard & Poor's 500. The line running through it is the earnings of the stocks that comprise the S&P. Before 1998, the S&P traded at a slight discount to its earnings trend. After 1998, it traded at a premium to its earnings. I believe this occurred because investors felt that a great growth spurt in earnings would occur and the price of stocks would be justified. It worked. From 1999 through 2000, earnings accelerated and then peaked. In anticipation of the peak, stocks began to trend lower.

If I believe that earnings will be flat for a while, it would be reasonable to assume that stocks should trade fairly close to the trend line. I also believe that stocks will begin rising again before earnings rise. Again, investors will buy based on where they think earnings are headed six months from now.

WHAT TO DO IF YOU SEE THESE TRENDS

Be Early to the Party—It Costs Too Much to Be Late: A Few Shortcuts

When you begin to see a base forming, it is always better to be early to the party than miss it. This means stocks will move in anticipation of the next market rally.

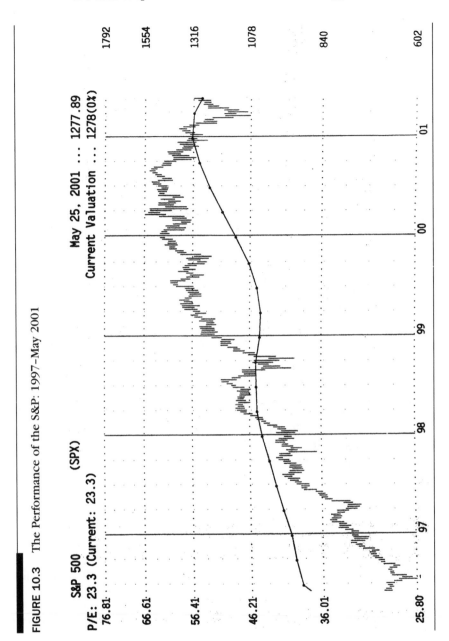

FIGURE 10.3   The Performance of the S&P: 1997–May 2001

THE SMART WAY TO REALLOCATE

Many clever mathematical formulas exist regarding reallocation. Although these may be good, they are simply too exhausting to follow. Further, I think my strategy works just as well.

First, find the areas where you are grossly overweighted. I assume these would be various growth sectors (as this discussion is prebear). For purposes of this discussion, overweighted means that these sectors are the largest pieces of your portfolio.

▬▬▬
RULE Immediately trim all stocks representing 15 percent or more of your portfolio down to a maximum of 10 percent.

Even if one stock is the greatest in the world and your best holding, trim it!

Through stop techniques (discussed later in greater detail), begin to place sell stop orders on stocks you may own in overweighted sectors. Rather than placing stops on all the stocks within these sectors, place stops only on the stocks you feel are most overpriced or most vulnerable to the bear market.

Follow the ⅓, ⅓, ⅓ Principal While Reallocating Your Cash

As the stops hit and stocks are sold, you will be building cash. Don't simply reallocate all your cash. Be patient. If a bear market is truly coming, you will probably be able to buy many more stocks cheaper and you'll wish you had some cash.

Begin to allocate the cash into the sectors that you are least exposed to and the ones that you think will perform well during the trough.

Ken Stern's School of Common Sense Allows Aggressiveness Now

Should you anticipate a rally in the market, this is the sixfold plan of attack:

1. Allocate funds as you would if we were in a trough phase of the business cycle.
2. Review your dream team stocks and determine if any are worthy buys.
3. Decide which stocks you feel will have the best sales and earnings as the economy strengthens.
4. Consider aggressive moves such as conservative use of margin for a small portion of your aggressive portfolio.

5. Laugh when the newspapers print doom and gloom stories.
6. Stick to your discipline and don't second-guess yourself.

Using margin to invest is one very aggressive play that can yield high returns—or cause an investor to lose money fast. When opening a brokerage account, investors usually have the option of investing on margin; in other words, the brokerage firm allows you to borrow money that could (should) be used to buy stocks.

Although margin requirements at different firms may differ, the concept is fairly similar. If you invest $50,000 in a brokerage account, the firm will lend you an additional $50,000. So now you conceptually have $100,000 to invest. If you invest the full $100,000 and make 30 percent, you have $130,000. If you decided at that point to cash everything in and pay off your margin balance (assume it's $50,000 plus $2,000 in interest), you will net about $78,000 (excluding transaction fees). So though you made 30 percent, in reality the percentage return is much higher based on the amount you invested. You basically doubled your return, or made almost 60 percent!

Of course, nothing is too good to be true. Here's the catch. First you must pay interest on the borrowed money—and the interest rate is usually not cheap. Assume the interest rate equals an annual percentage rate of 8 percent. Then assume you lose 20 percent on your investments over the course of one year, so in reality you would be losing 28 percent.

The second problem is a *margin call.* If you invest $50,000 and borrow $50,000, chances are the brokerage firm will want you to keep a balance of 50 percent equity to 50 percent loan balance. Easy, when stocks are going higher. But what if your portfolio drops to $80,000. The brokerage firm has the right to ask you to cough up more money, in this case an additional $20,000 to get back to 50 percent loan-to-equity value. If you don't have the cash, the brokerage firm has the right to sell stocks (probably at depressed prices) to satisfy the margin call.

This type of investing is very aggressive. Should you consider it, I recommend not taking out a very large margin: 10 to 20 percent of your total portfolio at a maximum.

Stick to Your Discipline and Don't Second-Guess

You may be absolutely correct in your research. You may find great investments and call the market direction correctly. But two problems can occur at this point. Either you don't make the investment because you second-guess yourself, or you make it and second-guess yourself.

Let's say you make the investment, but the stock doesn't move or it's going down. If you bought it to be a long-term core holding, buy more. Remember, I always believe core holdings should be bought three times over a fixed period of time, say three months.

If you bought the stock for a trade, place a sell stop on the stock immediately when you purchase it. The sell stop should be just below the stock's last support level or decide how much you are willing to lose on the trade. Assume you place a sell stop at a price 15 percent below what you purchased the stock for. If you are stopped out, you're out. Stop worrying about the stock, or continue to track it to see if it drops to a point you are willing to trade it again.

SUMMARY

I highly doubt that stocks would enjoy the phenomenal returns that they do without bear markets. There have been many periods when the market has averaged 10 percent, 12 percent, or even 15 percent. The risk premium is bear markets. But if we know they are coming, if we prepare for them, both with education and psychologically, we can make great investments and beat the bear.

As confusing as you and I may make it seem, it really is not all that confusing. Here is your pocket cheat sheet.

- Use indicators to call the market bottom.
- Decide which sectors you wish to overweight.
- Begin making investments in those sectors.
- Be aggressive only with the high-risk portion of your portfolio.
- Focus on your research, not the media.
- Look for companies that are ready to break out.

World-Class Stock Picking

PART FOUR

CHAPTER ELEVEN

The Power of Knowledge and Where to Find It

"Knowledge is power but only if a man knows what facts not to bother about." —Robert Lynd

We have talked about the economic cycle, and about top-down analysis for determining which sectors to own and when. We reviewed strategies for beating both the Standard & Poor's 500 and bear markets. We did this without analyzing one stock. Now, it's time to pick great stocks.

I assume you know on which sectors you wish to concentrate, which is irrelevant for this chapter. All we care about now is how to analyze companies.

Many disciplines exist for finding great stocks.

- *Momentum investors* look for stocks that are gaining strength when large amounts of people begin to invest in them.
- *Technicians* look only at charts to determine which stock looks as though it will appreciate. Technical investors often don't even know what the company they're investing in does to make money.
- *Value investors* want to be sure they are buying the company for less than its value would be if it were a private company.

This book is not an objective view of each style; other books can tell you about the different investment styles that exist. This book is about my discipline, which uses many of the techniques from various styles. But what is most important is that at the end of the day I want to know if I got a good deal on the company I bought. I will rarely invest unless I can tell you why this company is going to be worth more five years from now.

RULE Don't invest in a company unless you can state why this company will be more valuable five years from now.

Sector rotation and preparing for a bull market are absolutely necessary to my discipline. I think they help reduce my risk and make money for me more quickly. But what if I'm wrong? If I'm wrong, I can still sleep well at night knowing I own a piece of a great company. If this is true and I diversify among enough companies, my biggest risk is time: waiting out the cycle. So when it's all said and done, finding the best companies that have either the greatest growth prospects or paying the best price for the company is what matters most to me.

My advice for commonsense investing in a nutshell requires asking the following questions:

- Are you getting a good deal for the stock?
- If you are not getting a good deal, is the company worth paying a premium for? That is, will it experience phenomenal growth?
- Is this the right time to buy?
- Is this the right time to sell?
- Does the potential reward outweigh the risks?

Although I don't want to be pigeonholed, my investment discipline closely resembles what is known as G.A.R.P. (Growth At Reasonable Prices). I want companies that have growth potential, but I don't want to overpay for this growth.

RULE Treat every investment you make as if you were buying the company.

To do this, follow these steps.

- Step One—Determine what the company is worth today.
- Step Two—Determine if the reward outweighs the risk.
- Step Three—Determine what price you are willing to pay.
- Step Four—Stay informed.
- Step Five—Maintain a sell discipline.

To determine what a company is worth, I use fundamental research. To determine the right time to buy or to sell, I use both fundamental and technical research. I believe astute investors use any resources at their disposal to help work through the process of finding, investing in, and ultimately selling a winning investment.

WHERE TO GET INVESTMENT IDEAS

You can find ideas for investments in many ways and in many places, including these:

- Modeling and stock screening
- Where you shop
- Talking to friends, vendors, salespeople
- Reading business magazines, industry magazines, and general publications
- On the Internet

In addition, have a genuine curiosity. Watch TV for clever ad campaigns and for business news. If an ad catches your attention, maybe it's catching other people's attention too. This could help a company's revenues, which in turn could help the stock.

WHERE TO FIND INFORMATION ABOUT A SPECIFIC COMPANY

- Call the company.
- Call an analyst.
- Call a broker.
- Place yourself on the company's press release list.
- See if the library has Value Line or Standard & Poor's research reports.
- Check Internet sites.

Awesome Web Sites

The power of the Internet is amazing. Almost everything I talk about, and a large portion of the research I do, is available on the World Wide Web.

Sometimes you will use the Internet to screen stocks. Other times you will use it to track your portfolio. The Internet is able to provide historical company data, alert you if a company you're tracking (or own) makes news, provide technical charts and graphs, illustrate economic data—and this is just the beginning!

Here are a few of the sites I find most helpful. I am sure there are many more; this is merely the start of what I am sure is a remarkable list.

Stock Research

- <WWW.IBBOTSON.COM>
  This site has awesome historical market data and incredible software; it's used mainly by investment professionals.
- <WWW.ZACKS.COM>
  This site has the ability to create a portfolio, create a custom stock screen, or use a preset screen. (This is going to be very important and helpful in the next chapter.) Zacks has a sensible methodology for ranking stocks. I find the backtesting feature helpful.
- <WWW.INVESTOOLS.COM>
  This is one of my favorite sites for screening individual stocks. In addition, the stock reports aren't too shabby either.
- <WWW.BRIEFING.COM>
  This site has analysts that track and research stocks and the markets. The research is well thought out and timely. Many brokerage firms that research stocks have a potential conflict of interest because the companies they are researching may also be clients. Briefing does not do any investment banking, virtually squelching any conflicts. Briefing rates sectors as well.
- <WWW.FIRSTCALL.COM>
  This site is a must for investors who wish to track earnings projections of a company. First Call compiles statistics on all the analysts covering a company and provides an excellent commentary on possible earnings revisions for coming quarters.
- <WWW.VALUELINE.COM>
  This is another excellent source of fundamental and historical data about companies.
- <WWW.MORNINGSTAR.COM>
  This site is simply the best for mutual fund research for individual investors.

- <WWW.STANDARDANDPOORS.COM>
  There's more education here than you could imagine!
- <WWW.REFDESK.COM>
  This is a portal for many business and nonbusiness sites, including Bloomberg.
- <WWW.BLOOMBERG.COM>
  This is a great site for daily tracking of news and information on various markets.
- <WWW.MULTEX.COM>
  Just about all the fundamental and technical information you ever need to know can be found on this brokerage firm research site.
- <WWW.10KWIZARD.COM>
  Reading the annual and quarterly reports of a company can be very revealing. You can see if the company's gross sales are increasing, or you can research a particular industry. You can also track earnings, debt, and a multitude of other things.
- <WWW.BESTCALLS.COM>
  As an individual investor, you may not be able to meet with the management of various companies. Never fear, this site will patch you into management conference calls that are usually made after an earnings announcement or other important developments.
- <WWW.HOOVERS.COM>
  Stock-screening tools, news about IPOs, and much more can be found on this site.
- <WWW.YARDENI.COM>
  Ed Yardeni is the chief investment strategist at Deutsche Bank/Alex Brown. His sight offers excellent economic updates, historical data, and a superior macroview.
- <WWW.NDR.COM>
  Incredible historical market data helpful to spot trends and sector rotations can be found here.
- <WWW.MSN.COM>
  Another of my favorites, this site, which is very easy to navigate, offers timely financial news, stock quotes, a mutual fund directory, an advisor finder, money-saving tips, and the ability to track your portfolio. It also works as a personal finance site.

Initial Public Offering (IPO). When a private company goes public (offers ownership in the company to the public), the shares begin trading on a stock exchange.

- <WWW.REUTERS.COM>
  This is the best site for up-to-date news and information.
- <WWW.CNBC.COM>
  Great commentaries are on this site.
- <WWW.SMARTMONEY.COM>
  You can find all kinds of information on this fascinating site, from articles on home remodeling pitfalls to a map of the market that provides information on 600 different stocks at the click of a button. The site contains editions of *SmartMoney* magazine and links to other financial Web sites. There are areas for tracking your portfolio, news articles, a sector tracker, stock quotes, a bill payment center, financial calculators, and Smart-Money University, which is a basic primer on investing. This site is definitely worth reviewing.

Personal Finance Sites

- <WWW.QUICKEN.COM>
  I like this site most for personal finance information (ideas to pay off debt and retirement planning). I also like it's portfolio-tracking ability. Most sites have financial calculators, as does Quicken's. If you have the data available (net worth, debt, age, and retirement goals), you can prepare a balance sheet, retirement plan, and debt payoff plan within a couple of hours. You can also save the data and refer back to it to make changes or see what actions you need to take now to be where you want to be when you retire.
- <WWW.YAHOO.COM>
  The finance site at Yahoo! allows you to track stocks, create a portfolio, and access news and quotes. One of the features I particularly like about this site is its ability to graph the performance of individual stocks quickly and easily.

Stock Exchange Sites

- <WWW.AMEX.COM>
  This is the Web site for the American Stock Exchange. It lists quotes, the ticker, news, exchange-traded funds, earnings information, and a variety of other topics.

- <WWW.NYSE.COM>

  This site is a little different from the ones I've discussed so far. It offers many of the features the others do, such as news and market information, but it doesn't allow portfolio tracking or individual customization. There is information on this site about the operation of the New York Stock Exchange (NYSE) and the rules that regulate it. It also has a complete listing of all stocks on the NYSE and a section that describes the trading floor. If you've never seen the trading floor, you might find this enjoyable.

- <WWW.NASDAQ.COM>

  This site offers many of the features that Yahoo!, MSN, and Quicken offer. There is also a section on "Professional Investor Tools" that gives you access to a "Guru Stock Screener," a fund screener, and Nasdaq's list of the top 25 funds.

Television

Television is a valuable and easy-to-use source of timely information. When I'm sitting at my desk, I usually have a TV turned on at a low volume to some of the shows that cover the markets. If I hear something important, I can stop what I'm doing and focus for a few minutes on the news, which allows me to immediately act on information that affects my clients' or my own portfolios.

CNBC

CNBC is a 24-hour business news cable channel. Throughout the day, anchors and reporters interview analysts and traders from the various exchanges, and the station presents informative shows at regularly scheduled times. For a complete listing of CNBC coverage, go to <www.cnbc.com> or consult your local TV guide.

CNNfn

This is another 24-hour business news cable channel. Like CNBC, this one has regularly scheduled shows throughout the day that update you on many aspects of the economy and the markets. You can find a complete listing of these shows at <www.cnnfn.com> or check your local listings.

Bloomberg Morning News

This daily half-hour show airs each weekday morning on public television. It covers market activity for the previous day in addition to stock recommendations, interviews with money managers and analysts, and other financial information. You can find a local public television channel that carries *Bloomberg Morning News* at <www.bloomberg.com/tv/public.html>.

Wall $treet Week With Louis Rukeyser

Another half-hour public television show, this one shown weekly, is informative but still entertaining. Money management professionals are interviewed and a rotating group of panelists vote on how they think the market will move over the next three months. For a local listing, visit <www.pbs.org>.

Local News Broadcasts

Most major cities have a local financial editor/reporter who does daily updates on the markets and the economy. Shop around on your local news stations and see who you like. Remember, though, that the stations listed above generally have round-the-clock coverage, so their information will be more timely than waiting for a local news show.

Periodicals and Newspapers

OK, I know I said you would be reading yesterday's news. But sometimes there is a wealth of knowledge to be gained by looking at what the experts said yesterday and what actually took place. So there is value to having a few select subscriptions. Here are some of my favorites.

The Wall Street Journal (WSJ)

The Wall Street Journal
800-568-7625
<www.wsj.service@ dowjones.com>

This is undoubtedly the leader in printed material about the markets. Published on weekdays, the *WSJ* covers financial, political, and world news, features corporations and industries, and covers the previous day's activity in the markets. The *Journal* contains a column, "Heard on the Street," that has been known to have an impact on any stocks that are mentioned in it. The *Journal* is also offered online.

Barron's

Barron's is published weekly, on Mondays, by Dow Jones & Co. Geared toward the experienced investor, *Barron's* is a cross between a newspaper and a magazine. Along

Barron's
212-416-2700
<www.dowjones.com>

with feature articles and handy pull-out guides, it covers the market news for the previous week.

Investor's Business Daily

Most of this recent addition to the financial world (it began publication in 1994) reflects the investment philosophy of its founder, William O'Neil. The first two pages have news stories on recent market events,

Investor's Business Daily
800-831-2525
*<www.investorsbusiness
daily.com>*

but the rest focuses on helping readers make better investment choices.

Money

Offering coverage of all areas of financial planning, *Money* magazine covers investing, saving, retirement planning, spending, and tax preparation. *Money* also

Money
800-633-9970
<www.money.com>

includes "Investing 101" for the new investor and frequent lists of top-performing stocks, funds, and money managers.

Fortune

This magazine is both a business and investing periodical. Well known for some of its business rankings, including the Fortune 500, it offers in-depth views on companies

Fortune
800-621-8000
<www.fortune.com>

and industries. It also includes short articles on investment strategies and financial planning advice.

Kiplinger's Personal Finance

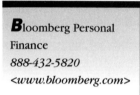

Kiplinger's Personal
Finance
800-544-0155
<www.kiplinger.com>

Containing four color-coded sections, this periodical primarily covers investment ideas. The sections include "Ahead," which contains short news articles; "Investing," which covers stocks, mutual funds, and industry sectors; "Managing," which covers financial planning; and "Spending," which covers equipment that can be used to enhance your office.

Bloomberg Personal Finance

Bloomberg Personal
Finance
888-432-5820
<www.bloomberg.com>

Containing a mix of news, financial data, and feature articles, *Bloomberg Personal Finance* also offers investment ideas and educational articles.

SUMMARY

Research and data are among an investor's best friends. Find out what's out there. Begin bookmarking these sites. Play with them and with all the other research available. Find out which ones are helpful and easy to use, and disregard the rest.

Be wary of information overload. No doubt you'll hear people talking about the same stock—one person may suggest a buy, the other a sell. One economist may say the economy has bottomed, the other that it is still trending lower. Don't allow yourself to become frozen into indecision with all this information. If you use *your* indicators, if you use *your* research, it will be much easier to sift through the volumes of information now available.

I read commentaries on the Internet. I call brokers and ask for their research reports. But usually it is *after* I have already decided where we are in the economy, which sectors I want to invest in, what macrotrend I'm favoring, and which stock screens I choose to run. What I now seek is any additional information that will either add to the position I have already taken or alert me to something I may have overlooked.

CHAPTER TWELVE

Create Winning
Stock-Picking Models

"The patient investor realizes a profit on his investment, whereas the only thing the impatient investor realizes is his mistake." —Unknown

Once an investor finds a desireable stock, several tests are available to determine if it is a worthy buy. But first, we have to find the stock. Talking to friends, reading, and all of the other suggestions I've mentioned are viable alternatives. One of my favorite ways, however, is through creating a stock screen and modeling a stock.

Modeling and screening can be done at the library, through publications, or on the computer. Financial advisors can be a great source to run screens for you. Finally, excellent screening techniques can be created through the products and services you may come in contact with everyday. Several Internet sites mentioned in the previous chapter allow you to select stocks—you plug in the variables and voila! Out pop the stocks that fit your criteria.

The problem is information overload. What should be screened and how it can be done quickly is the focus of Chapter 12.

MY FAVORITE FOUR STOCK-PICKING MODELS

Bottom-up investing is scouring the stock universe in an attempt to find stocks that match your criteria. Regardless of what the economy

PE *(Price-Earnings Ratio). This is also known as the* multiple, *the price of a stock divided by its earnings per share that gives investors an idea of how much they are paying for a company's earning power.*

is doing, forgetting sector rotation and most other criteria, when a stock hits a buy target a bottom-up investor will likely buy.

When you read the chapter on discipline, it will provide a bit more insight on my next statement. Previously, I discussed being in the right sectors at the right time. This is one discipline I adopt. Another discipline I adopt is sticking to one of my bottom-up stock picking models and buying *regardless* of what the market or the economy is doing. In fact, at times the two disciplines dramatically contradict. I like buying cheap stocks (upbringing). All three of my favorite screens have an element of cheapness. Stocks are probably cheap for a reason—it is probably the wrong time to buy the stock. Home building stocks might come up on my screen when interest rates are terribly high and nobody is buying homes. Recently, a certain drug stock appeared on my value model. It appeared because investors were worried about this drug company's growth prospect. It is easy to question things like future growth. However, the model spit it out and, while rumors were vicious, there was enough evidence to the contrary, so I swam upstream and bought it. Incidentally, the stock is Merck and so far the investment is doing rather well, thank you.

When using models to identify stock prices, remember to stick to your discipline (like everything in investing). When a model gives you ideas, explore them. Throw out whatever doesn't make sense, but learn to tune out all the reasons why the stock is and should be down and instead question what might make the stock rise. One criterion I have used successfully is to go back and find patterns of stocks that made money in past years. For example, in 2000, over 300 stocks doubled in price. (Not bad, considering most major stock market averages were down.) Many of these 300 stocks had common characteristics. I determine what these common characteristics are and then create a screen to show which stocks have these characteristics. I call this a historical growth model.

Historical Growth Model Characteristics

- Minimal downward earnings revisions. (During a bad economy, search for companies that are not earning less.)

- PEs did not exceed a 90 percent average PE to their industry. (It's important to find good companies, but by not paying over 90 percent to the industry, it helps assure me I am not overpaying for the stock.)
- Companies with at least three years of earnings, with a company earning a little more every year. (Selecting companies with at least three years of earnings helps reduce the risk of looking at start-up ventures. A little earnings increase every year shows me that a company can earn even more money as it grows.)
- Positive revenue growth. It always makes sense to invest in a company that can sell more of its products every year for at least three years.

Contrarian Model

Contrarian models are somewhat tough for many investors to digest, but they do make sense. I think you will find that sticking with this model will be fairly rewarding.

If you can find a stock that has underperformed the market for more than a 12-month period, chances are it was the wrong economic cycle for that stock and the stock was out of favor. Perhaps bad news (such as a negative earnings report) negatively affected the stock. But if the stock slowly begins to outperform the market (even slightly), it could mean that most of the bad news is out and is already reflected in the stock's price.

You further whittle your potential stocks down by not overpaying for a stock. If you pay a maximum of 80 percent of what its past three-year historical PE has been, you are not overpaying.

To really toughen up the screen, insist on a company whose profit margin has not dropped over the past year. It's a stellar feat if a company drops, for whatever reason, but maintains its profit margin. Once you've gone through this process, you will probably be left with only excellent, quality companies.

> *Insiders. Top management of a company or share-holders who own more than 5 percent of total shares outstanding.*

Next, determine if insiders are buying the stock. Your list is going to uncover some incredible ideas. If you still want to cut the list of companies even further, screen out stocks that are increasing their volume during up days as opposed to down days. This is a very important criterion. When markets fall, most stocks tend to fall. But minimal volume just means the selling is due to the market as a whole, not an individual stock issue. A very positive signal is when the stock is being purchased during up days.

On any given day, show stocks that have positive buy recommendations as well as a positive trend during a negative market.

Characteristics of a contrarian stock model include:

- Stocks that have underperformed the market by more than 30 percent over a 12-month period beginning 18 months ago.
- Stocks that have outperformed the market over the past six months, but by no more than 5 percent.
- Stocks with a current PE of less than 80 percent of the past three-year earnings per share (EPS) growth rate. (For example, if a company is growing earnings at a rate of 10 percent per year and the PE equals 10, an investor is paying 1 times the future growth of the company. This is called a PEG [price to earnings growth]. If the stock were trading with an 8 PE, it would be roughly equivalent to 80 percent of the future growth of the company, assuming the company was growing at 10 percent.)
- Stocks with a profit margin percentage that did not fall over the past year.
- Stocks with recent insider purchases that are greater than insider sells.
- Stocks whose average volume during their up days over the past three months is greater than their average volume during their down days.

Deep-Value Model

I enjoy screening stocks for deep value, similar to the contrarian indicator in that the screen will probably reveal stocks with problems. We are not looking for oceanfront real estate. We are looking for a stock whose price has dropped below the price that the bad news would justify and below what the price should reasonably be. Even if there is bad news about the stock, only three things can really happen: (1) The company can turn around and get better; (2) the company can get bought out; or (3) the company can go out of business. Try to buy only stocks that you think will play out in the first two scenarios. Don't buy the ones that you think will go out of business.

One example of a stock that would have hit the deep-value screen in 1998 is Philip Morris. As the markets crashed, this stock rose to new highs, more than doubling in price. As a result of the lawsuits against smoking, it was a deep-value model.

If a company's PE is very low compared to its historic average, yet is still paying a dividend, that proves to me that the company has earnings and a chance of succeeding. Further, revenues that equal earnings growth (even if it is only 1 percent) show the company has the ability to produce earnings and revenue growth. Further, a company that has cash flow helps prove to me that the company is probably not going out of business and might be an attractive acquisition target. Finally, I always look for profits and low debt if any stocks are left on your screen. Too much debt can sink a company pretty darn fast.

Characteristics of a *deep-value stock model* include:

- A PE less than long-term earnings
- A market PE less than 0.5
- Positive historical dividend growth
- Earnings growth greater than the market's
- Revenue growth in line with EPS growth
- Trading at less than one times sales
- Free cash flow at least 50 percent higher than earnings
- Net profit in excess of 10 percent
- Debt-to-equity ratio of less than 0.15

THE KEY TO STOCK SCREENS

Let's assume you find some excellent candidates by creating stock screens. The objective of a stock screen, after all, is to weed out companies you absolutely don't want. Once the screen reveals the best of the best, do more research. If you find one company that looks great but you later hear that it just lost its CEO or lost a major lawsuit, weed it out.

Although I suggested weeding out everything but the best of the best, as you know I don't recommend buying just one stock. Investing is very much a probability game. To place all your money on one bet isn't sensible. Instead, consider buying perhaps five stocks and consider placing a stop on all five. Let's assume, too, that you get stopped on three stocks with a 20 percent loss. Let's assume you only gain 10 percent, yet the remaining two stocks increase by 30 to 40 percent. Your overall return is excellent and your losses are minimized. Had you simply bet on one stock, you wouldn't have had the numbers on your side.

Previously, I talked about the wisdom of buying sectors instead of, or in conjunction with, individual stock purchases. Once you have committed to a strategy of buying individual stocks, diversification is a must. However, let's assume all the stocks that keep appearing through your screening process belong to one sector. It may make sense to buy the sector instead of individual stocks.

HOW YOU CAN CREATE A MODEL ON YOUR OWN

It's true that I have powerful software to create my models, but many Internet sites do much of the same screening. Flip back to the previous chapter and experiment with some of those sites.

Of course, you can always create a model on a spreadsheet. The problem is that you need to find the relevant data from one source or another. One of the best places for information is the Internet. So get wired! If you are not wired you will need to manually sort through many different stocks. Use the information and questions in Figure 13.4 as a guide. If you find a stock you like, you must compare it to other stocks in the same industry. Companies like Value Line categorize their research reports by industry. An investor would benefit by going to the library, pulling a Value Line report and researching *all* the stocks in the sector.

SUMMARY

It may seem a little intimidating at first to start screening stocks, but I have found more undiscovered gems this way than through any other method. If you aren't sure which criterion to use, play with several. Create sample models and track them (before committing any real money). See which ones work best and which criteria you are using that seem to be common threads.

Some of the sample screens on the Web sites listed in the previous chapter are great ways to get started as well. Many of those Web sites allow you to create sample portfolios to track your ideas.

So what are you waiting for? Go create some models and portfolios!

CHAPTER THIRTEEN

One Dozen
Fabulous Fundamentals and
Bonus Stock-Picking Checklist

DECIDING WHAT A COMPANY IS WORTH TODAY

To decide what a company is worth, I'm going to use the following hypothetical example to gather fundamental data. Fundamental analysis is widely used when attempting to determine what factors fundamental to a company are important in estimating the value of the company.

This type of analysis could encompass accounting information when looking at sales and income data; and a study of management could be important as well. Even a comparison of this company with other companies in its industry is part of fundamental analysis.

To decide what a company is worth today, we start with four fundamental criteria:

1. Market capitalization
2. Intrinsic (or private market) value
3. Sales momentum and ratio
4. Earnings momentum and ratio

A CASE STUDY

It's easiest to learn these first four criteria through a case study. Let's assume that you're in the business of buying businesses, and your specialty is buying clothing and apparel stores. You've heard of a hip apparel company called Kasman (a fictitious company) that has the trendiest clothes, the best designs, great distribution, and sensible expansion plans. The best part is that the owners are willing to sell the company. The first question you might ask is, What is the cost?

Understand that every company you can buy stock in is essentially for sale. Fortunately, we can buy a fraction of a company instead of buying the entire company or all of the outstanding shares.

1. Market Capitalization

If you multiply all the shares outstanding by the current price of the stock, the result equals the market capitalization of the company. This figure represents the company's selling price—the market capitalization, or market cap—and is what it would cost you if you were willing to buy all the shares of the company for yourself.

2. Intrinsic Value

Many value investors try to find what a company would be worth if the company were simply a private company that didn't offer shares for sale. Ours is an attempt to find the true *intrinsic value* or *private market value* of the company. Classic value investors, such as Graham, Dodd, Gabelli, and Buffett, are famous for studying companies in an attempt to find their intrinsic values. Knowing the market cap of the company is an important step in determining if the company is currently selling for more or less than what investors believe the intrinsic value of the company to be. They would also look for the capitalization and discount rate.

> **I**ntrinsic Value.
> *Valuation determined by applying data inputs to a valuation theory or model; the resulting value is comparable to the prevailing market price.*

Assume Kasman states it is for sale with its market cap starting at $1 million. Is this a good or bad price? There's no way to determine this until you know a little bit more, so let's build a crude income statement. The first, and often most important, question in building the income statement is, What are the company's sales, or in other words, its revenue?

How much of the product was sold? This is also referred to as the "top-line" number, usually the first number on the income statement and reported before expenses are taken out. Many analysts view sales as an even better measure than earnings because it is pure, meaning it is

---

FIGURE 13.1   Crude Income Statement

Kasman Income Statement

Year 2000
REVENUE $700,000

---

hard to overstate or understate sales, whereas earnings can be manipulated based on many factors that make it a bit more difficult to analyze.

3. Price-Sales Ratio—Sales Momentum

So now that you know Kasman's 2000 revenue, a bit more of the story is revealed. You can determine how many times sales you are paying for Kasman. In this case, you are paying 1.4 times, or a price-sales ratio (PS) of 1.4. (Market cap/Sales = Price to sales.) Is this good or bad?

We can't really answer that yet because two more facts are needed. First, you need to know how fast the company has increased its sales and how fast it projects sales will increase in the future. Second, you need to know what other apparel companies are selling for. This is critical for several reasons. First, I assume you want to know if you are overpaying. This is similar to buying real estate. If you were to buy an apartment, even if you planned to keep it for a while, wouldn't you like to know what comparable real estate is selling for in the neighborhood? Second, chances are you will sell this company (or the stock) at some point in the future. You need to know the ratio buyers of this company or its stock would be willing to pay. As you can imagine, depending on the industry and rate of growth, the PS varies widely. Retailers tend to trade at a much lower PS when compared with a software company.

So let's find Kasman's historical and projected sales.

FIGURE 13.2   Income Statement with Historical and Projected Sales

Kasman Income Statement

	1998	1999	2000	2001 (est.)
REVENUE	$500,000	$575,000	$700,000	$880,000

This is pretty encouraging. Not only are revenues increasing, but they are also increasing at a higher rate every year. From 1998 to 1999, the PS grew over 15 percent, then 20 percent from 1999 to 2000, and an estimated 25 percent from 2000 to 2001. The percent increase in sales every year is termed *sales momentum.*

Without knowing comparables or how solid the projected revenue is, I'd say that so far Kasman looks like a good investment, based on the fact that I will have revenues equal to my investment in less than 18 months.

Let's continue with the income statement to find the expenses.

FIGURE 13.3   Income Statement with Expenses

Kasman Income Statement

	Year 2000
REVENUE	$700,000
EXPENSES	
Labor	150,000
Rent	80,000
Materials	225,000
Shipping	50,000
Promotions	20,000
TOTAL EXPENSES	$600,000
NET EARNINGS	$100,000

---

4. Price-Earnings Ratio—Earnings Momentum

After adding all the expenses, we find that the net earnings (let's assume it excludes taxes, depreciation, and other confusing factors), equals $100,000.

The market cap is $1 million. The earnings are $100,000. If the company is worth $1 million and the earnings are $100,000, the price divided by the earnings equals $10. Therefore, the price-earnings ratio (PE) is $10. One of the most important criteria to fundamental analysis is the PE. I hope you understand and use it. Is $10 a bad number? Similar to sales momentum, the answer is contingent on many other factors.

- What has the earnings growth of the company been and what is it projected going forward?
- What are other companies within the same industry selling for as measured by their PE?
- Is there room for management to expand earnings as the company grows?

As rudimentary as this case study may seem, this is exactly what Wall Street analysts (who are often paid millions of dollars) do to determine if an investment makes sense. For the next four fundamental criteria, I won't use a case study. It is better to simply explain various strategies and then go on to the next chapter and apply these criteria to real stocks.

What Does the PE Tell Me? The PE tells investors how much they are paying for the company's earning power. Young growth companies tend to have higher PEs. Companies with lower PEs tend to be established and pay higher dividends. How can this figure help you? If you are looking for dividends or income, look for lower PEs. If you are looking for the growth portion of your portfolio, go with a higher PE.

FOUR MORE FUNDAMENTALS

5. Cash flow
6. Book value
7. Return on equity (ROE)
8. Profit margin

Many investors and analysts use complicated formulas to determine cash flow, book value, return on equity, and profit margins of a company. Because these formulas have already been performed on virtually every publicly traded company, I don't focus most of my time on re-creating their formulas. Rather, I study their estimates to find patterns, anomalies, and value. When I'm comparing two similar companies, a major factor in deciding to choose one investment over the other is that one company has far more free cash flow.

5. Cash Flow

The cash flow of a company is one of the most important methods for valuing a business. Although cash flow is defined many different ways, I focus on net, or free, cash flow. What is left after expenses are paid is free cash flow. Although accountants argue with this statement (they get picky), I think of free cash flow as net earnings. With this cash flow the company can pay a dividend, buy other companies, or expand its business. And all of this can be accomplished without jeopardizing the business.

In valuing a business, you can use the projected future cash flow as a measure of determining the present value of the company. Let's assume that you aren't too mathematically inclined, and let's also assume that many other analysts have already done this. So instead of trying to mathematically determine the present value of a company, simply compare the cash flow of a particular company with its competitors. The stronger and more predictable the cash flow, the more valuable the company. If a company trades at a lower price–cash flow ratio than it's competitors, you may have found value in that company. (In the next chapter I work through specific examples.)

We already learned that price divided by earnings equals the PE. The higher the PE, the more a company must earn to justify its richer multiple. It's the same with cash flow. As an investor, I don't want to pay a high multiple (price divided by cash flow) unless the company is expecting to generate significant amounts of cash.

I am also interested in the ratio of cash flow to earnings—that is, how much cash premium (or discount) is generated versus earnings generated. For example, a cash flow–earnings ratio of 1.7 means that for every dollar of earnings a company generates, it is generating $1.70 of cash flow. Is this good or bad? Again, an investor must compare it to the historical data of how the company usually trades and compare it against its competition. However, the more cash a company can generate, the more I like it. Companies with cash flow have extra cash, which can help grow the company.

6. Net Tangible Book Value

The book value of a company should be its worth if you simply sold the pieces of the company. If you sold a company's real estate, equipment, name, or good will and then subtracted its debt, you would get the book value.

It's not very often that a company trades for less than its book value. When it does, investors must determine why the stock is lower than the actual breakup value of the company. It may be because of such factors as the death of the CEO, a management shake-up, a large debt coming due, or the loss of a key account.

Again, I use book value to compare one stock to another. Different companies trade at different ratios to their book value. Retail stocks trade closer to their book values, as it is easier to measure the goods and inventory of a retail company. Technology stocks have more ideas and patents that may have, on paper, a lower book value. The result is that technology stocks tend to trade at a higher price–book value ratio.

If a company's book value is $10 per share and it is currently trading at $20, you are paying two times book. First, look at book value for how cheap or expensive your investment is. If a stock traditionally sells for two times book and is currently trading at three times book, that may be a sign that the company is trading at the high end of the valuation range. Or if a company that trades at two times book is currently trading at book value, you may have found value. Perhaps one company wants to acquire another company trading at its book value, and perhaps the stock will rebound to two times book when the right market cycle occurs.

7. Return on Equity

If you were to invest in a printer with the objective of printing documents for people for a fee, you would want to know how much that printer would earn for you compared with what the printer cost. This is a basic definition of return on equity (ROE). For publicly traded companies, it is the after-tax profits available to the shareholders and is expressed as a percentage. You could determine ROE by dividing net income by the shareholders' equity.

The bottom line is that it makes sense to find companies with high ROEs because it means they have good profit margins and are making money. Obviously, certain sectors have better margins then others. Technology stocks tend to have a high ROE, but discount retailers have a low ROE.

"Historically, stocks with higher ROEs and higher margins have fared better during bear markets."

I will invest in low ROE stocks, but I do so sparingly. If a recession occurs and a discount retailer has a low ROE, is there a chance that the company could lose money or go out of business? Sure there is! So unless other compelling arguments exist, stick to companies with a high ROE.

8. Net Profit Margin

We all know what profits are. I like to look at the net profits of a company. If it sold $1 million worth of product and had $100,000 left, that's a 10 percent profit margin. Again, why invest in companies that don't have great profits or the possibility of great profits within a relatively short period of time? It's the opportunity cost in the fact that many companies do have great profits.

Remember the Internet craze? All these great companies like Amazon, priceline, and Yahoo! were attracting lots of people to their Web sites. They were even selling consumers lots of stuff. Lo and behold, we found that their business models were not widely profitable (at least, not yet). So the stocks went way up, then way down. You can't go wrong with profits.

THE FINAL FOUR FUNDAMENTALS

9. How good is management?
10. Peek into the future: what is the competition doing?
11. What barriers of entry does this company face?
12. What is the catalyst?

9. Management

General Electric is a phenomenal company because of management. Many great companies die as a result of poor management, and many mediocre companies prosper as a result of good management.

Research the track record of the company's management. Read its annual report, business plan, corporate memos, and press releases. Do you like what is being said? Do you like the tone?

Call various departments within the company. Do the employees seem well informed? Do they talk about the company in "we" terms or "they" terms? "They" terms is not a good sign.

10. Peek into the Future

Always find out what new goods and services a company has on the drawing board. As a company matures, its product cycle matures. If it doesn't have something great coming along, the company could lose its luster.

Peeking into the future means looking at sales trends, too. If you are looking at buying Compaq (CPQ), go to computer stores. Ask employees what they think of Compaq and if anyone is buying the computers.

What Is the Competition Doing?

Is the competition coming up with better products than the company you are researching, or is the competition announcing tough times?

During the 2000 market slowdown, people slowed down their buying of cellular phones. Stocks of cellular phone manufacturers, such as Motorola, Ericsson, and Nokia, dropped. But it looked to me as if the one company that actually didn't lose market share was Nokia, and that when the growth phase resumed, Nokia would be the stronger competitor.

11. Barriers to Entry

It is fairly easy to open a donut shop; the barriers to entry are minimal. However, if you have a brand name and a loyal following, barriers to entry are somewhat higher. This is exactly why companies like Krispy Kreme Donuts and Starbucks trade at premiums to other stocks in their sector. If you wanted to buy a great business (and had a few billion dollars to buy it), would you rather buy Dunkin Donuts or Krispy Kreme, and why? Krispy Kreme, because Krispy Kreme clients are devoted and loyal; and Krispy Kreme's management is fresh, excited, and in a growth mode. Would you pay more for Krispy Kreme? Probably so, because to re-create this company would be very difficult. As easy as it is to make donuts, the barriers to entry are simply too high.

12. Catalysts

What is going to cause a stock price to rise? Banks and insurance companies being deregulated was a catalyst in the banking industry. Deregulation could have driven the stock price. New management could be a catalyst. Even a fresh new marketing campaign could be a catalyst.

THE COMMONSENSE CHECKLIST

The following is a basic checklist you can use for analyzing stocks. The key is to find the criterion that you feel is most important and stick to it. Don't compromise your discipline, meaning that if you feel it only makes sense to buy companies with a history of three years of earnings, don't deviate—eliminate the stocks that don't have three years of earnings and move on to the next one.

FIGURE 13.4   Ken Stern's Commonsense, All-Inclusive, Stock-Picking Checklist

1. Why Does This World Need the Product and Service of the Proposed Company? Why Will We Need It Five and Ten Years from Now?

   Now: _____

   Five years: _____

   Ten years: _____

2. Why Is Its Product or Service Better Than the Competition's?

   _____

   _____

3. How Hard Would It Be to Duplicate What the Company Does (Barriers To Entry)?

   _____

   _____

4. Do the Potential Rewards Outweigh the Risks?

   Potential Rewards:

   _____

   _____

   Potential Risks:

   _____

5. Management

   Experience?

   _____

   Quality of its written reports (see its Form 10-K).

   _____

   _____

FIGURE 13.4   Checklist, *continued*

Employee turnover should be low.

Employee Turnover Rate: _____

6. Market Cap:

Allocate most of your investments to stocks with market caps over $1 billion.

_____

7. Channel Checks

Call vendors of products. Are sales going well? _____

_____

Talk to retail floor personnel. Are sales going well? _____

_____

Are competitors increasing sales?_____

_____

8. Sales/Earnings/Cash Flow (SEC):

Did company report quarterly SEC that exceeded the previous quarter for the same period?

_____

Have SECs increased at a faster pace each year for three years?   Yes No

Have the SEC increases been greater than the competition's?   Yes No

If not, what event occurred? (Sale of a business, recession, etc.)

_____

_____

_____

Why do you think SEC increases will continue or resume?

_____

_____

Is the company projecting SEC increases for the next two quarters?   Yes No

Insist on a minimum of three years of positive sales and earnings.

9. What are the price-sales ratio, price-earnings ratio, and price–cash flow ratio?

Price–Sales Ratio: _____

Price–Earnings Ratio: _____

Price–Cash Flow Ratio: _____

(continued)

FIGURE 13.4   Checklist, *continued*

Is this high or low compared with the company's historical average?
High Low

Is this high or low compared with its sector?   High Low

Is this high or low compared with its next biggest competitor?   High Low

Did sales exceed what was expected?   Yes No

10. Book Value

What is the price–book value of the competition? _____

What is the company's historical norm? _____

If the current book value is higher or lower than the norm, why? Are profits higher to justify a higher book value? Did the book value go down with the economy? _____

_____

11. Profit Margins and Return On Equity

As the company grows, are margins increasing? Try and stick to companies with net profit margins above 8% and ROEs above 10%. _____

_____

12. What Nonfinancial Factors Make This Stock Attractive?

Does the company have great name recognition? Do people love this company and are they loyal to it?   Yes No

Does it have a clever and effective marketing and public relations program?
Yes No   Notes: _____

_____

13. What Is the Catalyst That Will Allow This Stock to Move Higher?

Are volume and average daily trades increasing on the stock? _____

Is a new law going to affect the stock?   Yes No   How? _____

_____

Has new management been hired?   Yes No

Is a new product or service about to be launched?   Yes No

Product or service: _____

Are earnings and sales increasing at a faster pace than analysts expected?
Yes No

14. Based on Current and Next Period in the Business Cycle, Is This the Best Time for the Stock?   Yes No

---

FIGURE 13.4   Checklist, *continued*

15. Insider Transactions

    Are insiders buying or selling company stock? _____

    _____

    Does the company have a stock buyback program?   Yes No

16. How Does the Chart Look?

    Is the stock rising on higher volume?   Yes No

    Does it go down only on lower volume?   Yes No

    Is it breaking out of its 50-day moving average?   Yes No

17. Why Should This Stock Be Valued Higher Than It Is?

    Are analysts revising the company's earnings and sales estimates upward?
    Yes No

    Is the stock simply too cheap?   Yes No

SUMMARY

You now have all the fundamental and accounting knowledge necessary to make smart investments. Of course, you can always have more. But what you learned is enough to analyze and compare businesses. Now proceed and let's analyze some real companies.

CHAPTER FOURTEEN

The Right Way
to Compare Stocks

We invest to make money. We choose the stock that will make us the most money with the least amount of risk. If you had a choice between two cars that were very similar, including the price, with the only difference being that one was built to be safer, which would you buy? The safer one, of course!

The same is true for stocks. If two stocks are similar, but your research leads you to believe one is safer, it is only sensible to opt for the safer stock. If one stock appeared to be growing much faster but was valued at the same price as an alternative stock, you would choose the one that was growing faster.

Before I purchase any stock, I compare it against a competing stock and the industry as a whole. In the previous chapter we discussed how to find competing stocks in the same industry. If you don't know how to do this, review last chapter. When I do this comparison, this is what I look at:

- Price-earnings ratio compared with historic and future growth
- Current revenue models and future estimates
- Debt load
- Size of the company
- Key ratios
- The chart
- Intangibles

COMPARE HOME DEPOT AND LOWE'S

If you are having trouble finding any of the historical data I am using, the data is available in numerous locations.

Let's assume you were shopping in Home Depot the other day and thought it was a cool store. You go to its Web site and find that it is publicly traded. Before investing in the stock, however, you research competing companies, and you find Lowe's. Let's compare the two.

FIGURE 14.1   Comparison of Home Depot with Lowe's as of April 27, 2001, on Specific Measures

	Home Depot	Lowe's Capital	Sector (Retail– Home Improvement)
Symbol	HD	LOW	RTHOM
Stock Price	$48.10	$62.10	$3,978.65
PE	43.7	29.4	37.9
Earnings per Share—Percent Change			
Latest qtr (Jan 01)	Down 20%	Down 5%	(Mar 01) Down 4%
Latest 12 months	Up 10%	Up 18%	Up 4%
5-Year hist growth rate	29%	27%	24%
Estimated Earnings—First Call			
Current qtr (Apr 01)	Down 7%	Up 10%	(Jun 01) Up 3%
Year ending Jan 02	Up 12%	Up 15%	(Year ending Dec 01) Up 11%
Business Overview and Comments			
Home-improvement superstores			
Revenues—% change			
Latest qtr (Jan 01) . . .	Up 14%	Up 20%	(Dec 00) Up 10%
Latest 12 months . . .	Up 19%	Up 18%	Up 13%
Capitalization			
% Long-term debt to total capital	9%	33%	9%
Market cap ($ in billions)	$111.4	$23.8	$93.7
Key Ratios and Measures			
Dividend yield	.3%	.2%	.4%
Price-Book	7.4	4.3	6.2
Price–Cash Flow	35.1	19.5	29.0
Price-Sales	2.44	1.27	2.00
Cash Flow–Earnings	1.2	1.5	1.3
Return on equity (margins)	18.8%	15.9%	19.5%

Price-Earnings Ratio Compared with
Historic and Future Growth

We notice first that the PE for Lowe's (29.4) is lower than Home Depot's PE (43.7). The industry (Retail–Building Supply) supports a PE right in the middle of the two at 37.9. The question is why Home Depot's (HD) earnings are so high. Have the earnings been growing faster for HD to warrant this?

As illustrated in earnings per share, five-year historical growth rate, you see that HD has indeed grown 29 percent compared with Lowe's (LOW) 27 percent. I would say that this difference is not enough to warrant the spread in share price.

We also need to review the trading history of the stock. Has HD's PE been higher or lower in the past? Based on historical earnings data, it seems that both companies' earnings have been clipping along at the same pace over the last five years. It looks as though HD has historically supported a richer PE, or multiple. Perhaps this was because of its explosive historical earnings. Even though its PE is lower than historical norms, HD is still vulnerable because it is unlikely to continue to grow its earnings nearly as fast as in the past. Although I believe the same is true for LOW, the premium you are paying for LOW is not as high, despite the fact that its earnings growth has been about the same.

Notice also future growth (Estimated Earnings). If the analysts who track both of these companies are accurate, it looks as though LOW will earn far more than HD in the current quarter (April 2001) and will earn even more than HD for all of 2002.

If, in fact, LOW grows its earnings by 15 percent and you are paying a PE of 29.4 percent, you are paying a price–future earnings growth (PEG) roughly two times the future earnings growth rate of this company. Although it depends on the industry, I generally don't like to pay more than one and a half times future growth. In the case of HD, an investor is paying a PEG of more than three times! Remember that this is based on today's numbers. Go back to figure 14.1. Do you see PE based on estimated earnings? These estimates are provided by analysts who research these companies. They are projecting earnings to increase in 2002, and the PE automatically goes down if this happens. The PE is the price divided by the earnings, so if you input earnings higher than today's price (what is expected for 2002), you will know what the PE for the stock will be in 2002, so long as the stock doesn't move from today's price. If LOW does hit its numbers and has a PE of 21 times future earnings growth in 2002, I would say that, based on its historical trading pattern, its price is very cheap. (See Figure 14.2.)

The question is how comfortable you are with the earnings estimates. I feel it is better to buy a stock that looks fairly valued (based on historic norms) or cheap today and be pleasantly surprised tomorrow. Meaning, don't simply bet on the possibility of strong future earnings.

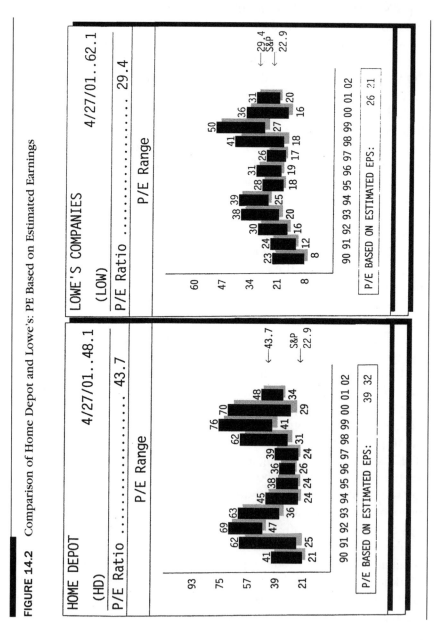

FIGURE 14.2   Comparison of Home Depot and Lowe's: PE Based on Estimated Earnings

Look at the value based on today's earnings. If that looks good then you can consider future earnings and decide if the company is still attractive.

So on a relative basis, HD is the more expensive company. LOW is more fairly priced compared with historic and relative values.

Revenue Growth and Ratios

As an investor, I need to see revenue—at least three years of increasing revenue. If revenue is currently down, why? Will it come back up? Am I getting the stock cheap enough to justify the investment?

I was surprised to see Lowe's revenues increasing by a higher percentage for the latest quarter than Home Depot's and almost the same (1 percent less) as HD's over the last 12 months. This does not mean LOW has more revenue; it means the revenue for the last quarter grew at a faster rate than HD's. So answer the question, "Am I getting either of these companies cheap based on how much the stock costs in relation to sales?"

Go to Key Ratios and Measures in Figure 14.1, scan down to price-sales, and notice that HD is trading at 2.44 times sales. That means if the company sold $1,000,000 last year, and someone wanted to buy the entire company, the selling price is $2,440,000. Sounds expensive, doesn't it?

In fact, my rule of thumb is to pay one times sales for companies growing their earnings at less then 20 percent per year. I will pay 1.5 times sales if they are growing revenue at over 20 percent per year. If they are growing revenue at over 50 percent per year, I may pay in excess of two times sales, but only on a case-by-case basis.

Remember that LOW's revenue has increased at about the same rate as HD's, but you will notice its PS is much less at 1.27. I don't find this cheap, but you'll notice that it is cheaper than the industry as a whole.

How Much Debt Does the Company Support?

Looking at Capitalization, HD is virtually debt free. I find this very comforting in volatile markets, especially in retail. LOW has 33 percent debt to total capital.

Until now, LOW has been looking like the lower-priced stock (in terms of the data presented), but 33 percent debt is high. At this point, I would find out if it plans to refinance its debt or pay some of it off and, if so, when.

How Large Is the Company?

When comparing companies, it is often thought that a larger company is safer. Many investors believe larger companies will weather periods of economic uncertainty easier because earnings and revenue won't be so sporadic. Investors often like to buy a leading and larger company, thinking the larger company could squelch its competition. I believe that when buying the leader is clearly indicated, even if the leader is more expensive, it is better to do so.

> *I prefer to buy the number two or three players in an industry.*

However, there is not always a clear argument for buying the larger company, as in the case of LOW and HD. I prefer to buy the number two or three player in an industry for a few reasons. One is that the larger company might buy out its competitor. I also like the smaller one if it is cheaper than the larger company and growing at a faster rate (as is the case in LOW versus HD). The third reason I would buy a smaller competitor is if I felt it had a better mousetrap—that is, a better product, service, or unique twist.

Capitalization

If you multiply the current price of a stock by the number of shares outstanding for a particular company, the resulting figure gives you the market cap of the company. Basically, that is what the company would be worth if you purchased 100 percent of the shares today.

As you can see from Capitalization in Figure 14.1, HD is much larger, with a market cap of $111 billion compared with a $23 billion market cap for LOW.

Key Ratios

LOW is trading at four times book compared with HD at seven times book. LOW is cheaper than both HD and the industry average of six times book.

LOW is also trading at a lower price-cash flow and a higher cash flow-earnings. Remember, we want a high cash flow-earnings, which means that for every dollar the company earns, it generates x number of dollars in cash flow. In the case of LOW, at a cash flow-earnings of 1.5, it generates 1.5 times cash flow for every $1 in earnings.

The Chart

Instead of creating a short-term technical chart, I wanted to see how these stocks were trading compared with a longer-term trend. Based on this, I made two five-year graphs and included the earnings trendlines (see Figure 14.3 and 14.4). It appears that both HD and

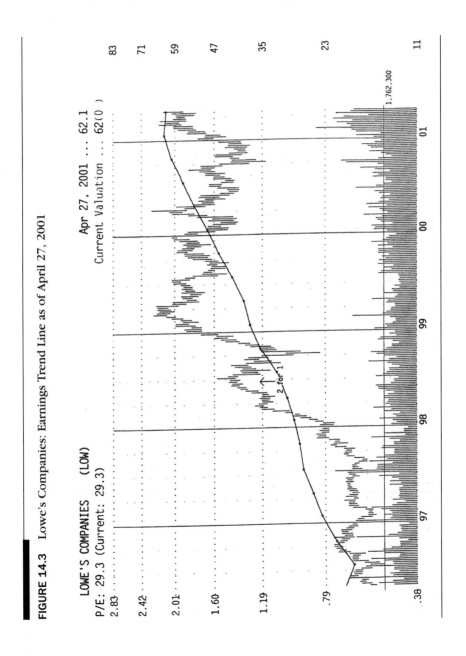

FIGURE 14.3   Lowe's Companies: Earnings Trend Line as of April 27, 2001

You don't know where to go to get the charts? Try <www.bigcharts.com>.

LOW were trading at a fairly close relation to their earnings trend line (slightly above it). Both have dropped below it, which may suggest, if earnings don't fall dramatically, the stocks could be undervalued compared with historical means.

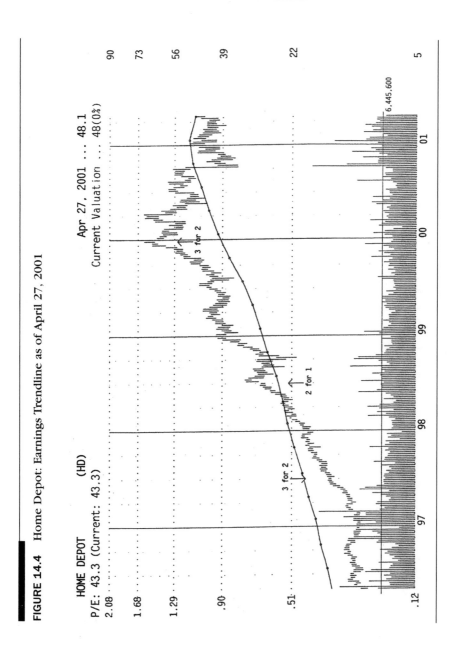

FIGURE 14.4   Home Depot: Earnings Trendline as of April 27, 2001

Intangibles

Of course, other factors go into deciding what is important when comparing stocks. Some of these are intangibles, which means, you can't put a price tag on the value of certain things. You can't put a price tag on the Coca-Cola brand name, for example.

Here are a few intangibles for LOW and HD.

- HD has better name recognition and more earnings stability.
- HD is the leader and sets the standard in home-building mega-stores.
- HD has a more visible and well-known management.
- HD is the number one player, whereas LOW is number two.

SUMMARY OF HOME DEPOT VERSUS LOWE'S

This fun exercise is one I do every day on a litany of different stocks. You'll notice that neither HD nor LOW is cheap based on my standards. If earnings and revenue exploded, they would be cheap, so I would seriously consider where I thought we were in the business cycle. I would seriously consider whether I thought retail spending would increase, decrease, or stay stagnant over the next few years.

During the recovery I lighten up on retail stocks considerably. However, after interest rates dropped their fourth time in April 2001, my associates and I started to believe retail stocks could see a pickup in time for Christmas. Further, with the building industry still strong and refinancing on an upswing, we felt the building industry might benefit.

Both LOW and HD are risky because their stocks are not cheap based on *today's* multiples; they will be a good investment only if they hit their earnings numbers for tomorrow. Based on these data, we slowly began investing in this sector. Although we invested in both companies, the data above suggested that LOW was the better-positioned stock for appreciation. I hope that by the time you read this, we will have been proved correct.

CHAPTER FIFTEEN

Know When to Hold and When to Fold

"Everybody wants to be a championship team, but nobody wants to practice." —Bobby Knight

It's bad enough to invest in a stock and watch it go down, down, down. But I think it is even worse to buy a stock and watch it charge ahead, only to see it subsequently plummet. Knowing when to buy, sell, and hold is a discipline in and of itself. Half the battle is finding a great stock. The other is deciding when to buy, sell, or simply hold.

Assume your portfolio consists of two parts: core holdings and uncommon opportunities.

RULE Sell your core holdings only if the reasons are overwhelming.

A core holding is a position that you believe anchors your portfolio. It is the type of stock that you could conceivably leave to your kids. It is an investment that you think should outperform the overall index through all market cycles. The rules for selling core holdings are as follows:

- Sell if any one stock reaches 15 percent of your portfolio. When this happens you have two choices: (1) sell 5 percent right away or (2) sell 5 percent over three months, one-third at a time on the same day every month—regardless of what the stock is doing that day. Don't try and guess the market. By selling on a preset date and time, you take your emotions out of the equation and hope to average a decent price over the three sells. If you don't do this, you may become greedy and get burned by waiting for a certain price, only to see the stock drop.

- Sell only if something dramatically changes with the stock. A dramatic change would be a company's product becoming obsolete or a serious loss in market share. A rule of thumb is if a company loses 15 percent or more market share without a reasonable explanation, reconsider this investment.
- Sell if the stock is terribly overvalued. Review the fundamental criteria. If the stock is seriously overvalued, place a stop loss on it. If it keeps going higher, raise your stop loss.

These would be the only times to consider selling core holdings. The remainder of your portfolio consists of uncommon values, which are investments you made for probably one of three reasons. The first reason is you thought the timing for the stock was right based on where you thought the economy was headed. Second, your fundamental research showed that the stock was incredibly undervalued. Or, third, the company is a leader (category killer) with a compelling business plan for superior growth in the next five to ten years. But you may be wrong, so you have two choices: sell or buy more.

RULE Never fall in love with a stock.

Buy it or sell it based on your research, the business cycle, and what your asset allocation model requires.

RULE Cut your losses and let your winners run.

RULE Begin selling stocks that are 25 percent to 50 percent higher than what you think is fair value or if the changing business cycle will affect the stock.

FAIR VALUE

Determining fair value is obviously not a simple task. I think a stock is expensive based on the following five criteria:

1. A stock trading at more than two times its future, long-term growth rate.
2. A stock's sales, earnings, and cash flow (SEC) ratios 30 percent higher than its competitors.
3. A stock trading at on excessive PS compared with its sales growth.
4. A stock trading 30 percent higher than its earnings trend line.
5. A stock that will be adversely affected by the next stage in the business cycle.

Obviously, this checklist is just a rule of thumb. If a company is showing increased sales and earnings, has a new product or technology about to be unveiled, or is affected by any other positive potential catalyst, I would rethink selling the stock.

USING STOPS TO SELL A STOCK

One trading mechanism available to us is a stop. A stop order is actually selling a stock at a certain price; if your stock hits that price, it's sold. Some investors place stops on the high end, meaning if they own a stock at $10 per share, they may place a sell stop order to sell the stock at $15. I *do not* agree with this type of stop. If you have a winning stock, let it run. If that $10 stock hits $15, it might go to $20.

I believe that if you think your stock is expensive and the only reason it keeps going up (in the short term) is because of Wall Street stupidity, place a stop to protect against downside. Wall Street stupidity occurs once a stock is trading at far too high a value based on my, or your, research. If Wall Street gets excited about a stock, it starts trying to buy the shares, and could trigger a mania that propels the stock to the moon. So long as the stock is going higher, let it run.

Find the *support level* of the stock. What price did the stock fall to during it's last low? If the stock breaks below that support, it could keep going down. If the support on the stock holds, then there is a good chance the rally of the stock will continue.

Consider the graph of General Motors (GM) in Figure 15.1. Starting in June 2000, the price of GM began falling. It fell to about $60 per share and then bounced up; in other words, GM found support at about $60. This support was tested briefly, held, and then the stock began climbing again. After peaking in the middle $70 range, it began falling again and dipped below the $60 support level—a negative

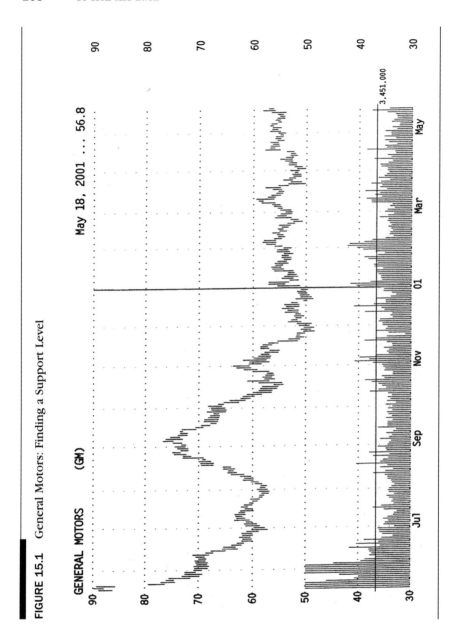

FIGURE 15.1   General Motors: Finding a Support Level

sign. Although it rebounded slightly, it quickly reversed course and dropped to $50, creating a new support level. Notice that since then it has been in trading between $50 and $60.

IF YOU STILL BELIEVE THE STOCK WILL GO HIGHER, DOUBLE DOWN

If you truly believe in a stock, especially a core holding, then ride out the turbulence. But if you have a stock that goes lower, never, ever say, "I am just going to wait until this stock gets back to where I paid and then sell it!" By saying this, you are reiterating the fact that you believe the stock is going higher. In essence, you are reaffirming a buy on this stock. So if you think it's going higher, double down. Buy more.

Assume you allocate 5 percent of your portfolio to XYZ company. The stock drops to half of what you paid for it, but you still believe in the company and still love its product and service. You believe the stock went down for the wrong reasons. If you allocated 5 percent of your portfolio to it, you now have only 2.5 percent of your portfolio invested in the stock as a result of the correction. Why not invest enough to get it back to 5 percent of your portfolio? Now, if the stock gets back to your original purchase price, you should make 33.33 percent on your money.

SUMMARY

Selling a stock is far more difficult than buying it. Investors get emotional about their holdings. Once a stock is bought, investors don't want to sell and lose money if it goes down. If the stock goes up, investors become greedy and believe the stock will rise forever.

Stick to your discipline—and your discipline should include a sell strategy. Even though many investors sing the praises of buy and hold, it doesn't make sense to hold forever. General Electric is the only stock still in the Dow Jones Industrial Average since its creation.

CHAPTER SIXTEEN

Building a Model Portfolio

"The more you study, the more you find out what you don't know; but the more you study, the closer you come."
—Cozy Cole

It's all starting to come together! Just think about how much knowledge you now possess. With this knowledge you can find information to determine what stage of the business cycle we are in, which stock sectors might perform well during each phase of the business cycle, analyze each one of the stocks within the sectors you like, and know when to consider selling a stock. The last step is deciding how to fit all of this into a model portfolio.

Asset allocation and *diversification* are discussed frequently but in many different contexts. Asset allocation may seem confusing because it can mean different things. There are three major phases of asset allocation. The first phase is determining the percentage of your assets that should be at risk (invested in stocks) rather than in safer investments such as bonds or cash. Your retirement plan and personal wealth formula are your guidelines for determining how much to allocate to stocks, bonds, cash, or other investments. Remember in Chapter 3 on the personal wealth formula (PWF) when I talked about the three-jar concept? You consider factors such as how long you plan to invest, your time horizon, income needs, and the like. Retirement planning is beyond the scope of this book, so to explore it further, see your financial planner or find another resource.

The second form of asset allocation deals with diversification within your stock portfolio. Without proper diversification, your risk is undoubtedly increased. Instead of using an abstract model to see this, just consider what happened from the late 1990s through the beginning of 2000. Many people (they call themselves investors—I call them gamblers) placed all their money in tech stocks. Regardless of the merits (or lack of) of investing in tech stocks, many of these investors lost everything when the bottom fell out of tech stocks.

This phenomenon is not isolated just to tech stocks; consider those investors that only invested in their company's stock, or utilities before deregulation, or bonds before interest rates jumped. Without proper diversification, investors will get burned.

The third form of asset allocation diversification is based on the business cycle.

BUILD A MODEL BASED ON
YOUR INVESTMENT DISCIPLINE

Assume that we wish to have two major types of investments in our equity portfolio: core holdings and uncommon opportunities. In such a case, here's my advice.

1. Pick six major sectors your research indicates will do well.
2. Decide which sectors you wish to overweight.
3. Buy at least three stocks within each sector.
4. On a monthly basis or as the business cycle changes or stocks become overvalued, rotate the sector weighting and stocks within each sector.

Consider the two pie charts in Figures 16.1 and 16.2. Figure 16.1 is the Standard & Poor's 500, and Figure 16.2 is going to be your portfolio.

Assume the economy is in a contraction. Pick the six sectors you wish to invest in: utility, health care, financial services, retail, technology, and consumer staples. Over-weight the first three, (as compared to the S&P 500) and underweight the second three. As the economy shifts, overweight or underweight your portfolio based on your data.

HOW MANY STOCKS DO YOU NEED?

Try to avoid allocating more than 5 percent of your portfolio to any one stock. Based on this criterion, you would have 20 plus stocks.

FIGURE 16.1   S&P 500 Holdings as of May 18, 2001

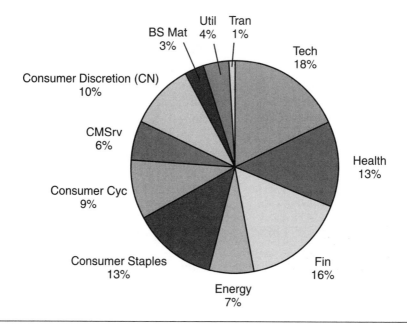

FIGURE 16.2   A Model Portfolio

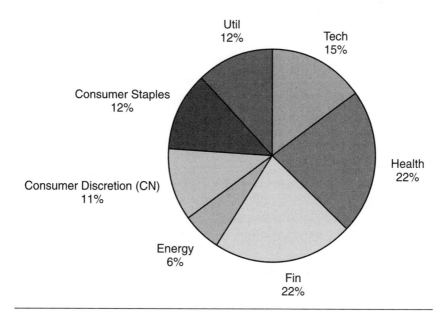

This could lead to costly transaction charges if you are purchasing less than a round lot (100 shares) at a time.

WHAT ABOUT DIVERSIFICATION BETWEEN STOCKS, BONDS, AND CASH?

You are going to invest different percentages of your portfolio in cash, bonds, and stocks depending on your PWF. The longer you have to invest and the longer you don't need the money, the more exposure to equities you can risk.

A good way to reduce risk, however, is to allocate between stocks, bonds, and cash. Although this sounds very simple, it's an extremely effective strategy for reducing risk and providing superior returns.

One-Third, One-Third, One-Third

1. Start with one-third of your money in each of the following; cash, bonds, and stocks.
2. Review your portfolio on January 30 of every year. If stocks or bonds drop, use enough cash to bring the level back to 33 percent in each asset category.
3. If stocks rise in value, sell enough stocks on January 30 of every year to bring the equity weighting back to 33 percent. Invest the proceeds in the asset class that lost money—bonds or cash. If neither lost money, add your returns to your cash.
4. Do the same thing if bonds rise in value.

I know this sounds basic, but it is a great way to keep risk down and very often beat the markets. Of course, this strategy doesn't take into account the negative effects of taxes and possible transaction costs.

AUTOPILOT INVESTING

I have discussed in previous chapters that autopilot (that is, automatic) investing is a must, not an option, for getting rich from a bear market. Instead of just trusting Ken Stern's School of Common Sense, I wanted to prove to you through a silly chart what my dad taught me eons ago.

Dad said, "You know, son, we have an Uncle Buck who is in the cattle business. And every year, for seven months during cattle-buying season, he buys cattle. The price of cattle is very volatile, and it's many a cattle farmer who loses his shirt if he loses his head.

"In fact, I remember one year when Uncle Buck said to his wife, your Aunt Martha, 'Martha, we are going to spend $1,000 per month for seven months on cattle this year.'" The first month cattle was going for $1,000 per head. Uncle Buck bought one head. "Wow," he said to Martha, "cattle sure is expensive this year." But something tragic happened. In just one month, because of mad cow disease, the price of cattle dropped in half. Uncle Buck was scared that he wouldn't be able to sell the cattle he had purchased. Nevertheless, he kept his head and used the next $1,000 to buy two heads of cattle.

If this wasn't bad enough, the third month came and cattle dropped again to $250. Uncle Buck said to Aunt Martha, "Honey, at this rate we won't be able to sell any of the cattle I buy. We'll be broke. Let's just take our losses and get out." Aunt Martha said, "Now Buck, we need the cattle. You said you would buy $1,000 worth per month. Be patient and stick to your discipline." And he did.

As the chart below illustrates, the price stayed down for a while and slowly moved back up. By the time the seventh month came, Uncle Buck was ecstatic that the price had gone back up to $1,000 per head of cattle (it turns out mad cow actually made his cattle worth more). Now Uncle Buck could sell all of his cattle and get his original investment of $7,000 back, right? Wrong!

While it is true that Uncle Buck invested $7,000, he owned 16 head of cattle. In fact, his $7,000 investment more than doubled to $16,000, but the price of cattle never exceeded his original investment.

FIGURE 16.3   Uncle Buck's Investment

Amount Invested	Price per Head of Cattle	Number of Heads Purchased
$1,000	$1,000.00	1
1,000	500.00	2
1,000	250.00	4
1,000	250.00	4
1,000	500.00	2
1,000	500.00	2
1,000	1,000.00	1
Total $7,000	$ 437.50	16

RULE Always be investing.

THE MORAL OF THE STORY

Uncle Buck's story is an example of autopilot investing. You *want* bear markets. You know that they are temporary and that the long-term trend of the market is higher. If you invest $1,000 in January and the price per share is $20, you bought 50 shares. If the price drops to $10 and you still invest $1,000, you would purchase 100 shares. If, in the third month, the price rises back to $20 and you sell the total 150 shares you own, you make out like a bandit.

World-class investors always invest. We are simply not smart enough to call the market right every time. If you are invested 100 percent in cash and the market rises, you lose. If you invest all of your money and the market drops, you lose. Our emotions often get in the way—we get either scared or greedy. We try and call market bottoms and market tops—and we're often wrong. Autopilot investing is a simple, thoughtless way to make money from a bear market and be a world-class investor.

SUMMARY

It seems that no matter how often investors are taught the same basic principles, they don't follow them. Asset allocation will help reduce your risk. It is sheer gambling and foolishness to place all of one's assets in any one asset class—regardless of whether that class is technology or utilities.

Asset allocation even touches on the oldest rule—*buy low, sell high*. The allocation strategy I previously mentioned suggested you take the asset category that has grown over 33 percent and sell a sufficient amount of it to reduce the portfolio to 33 percent. Then use the money to buy the sector of your portfolio that is down and no longer equals 33 percent.

This is an easy concept. Buy low. Sell high. Now why didn't we sell when stocks jumped up so much in 1999? And why didn't we buy more when they were low in 2001? Hmmmm.

CHAPTER SEVENTEEN

The Dogs of the Dow—
Is It Really That Easy?

It's so simple that it seems almost silly. Yet it works quite well actually. Based on my calculations, an investor would have averaged over 17 percent since 1973 by following this strategy. This compares to the Dow Jones Industrial Average's annualized return for the same period of less than 12 percent.

> **"An investor would have averaged over 17 percent since 1973 by following this strategy."**

The Dogs of the Dow is an investment system. After the stock market closes on the last day of a year, an investor searches for the ten stocks that have the highest dividend yield in the Dow Jones Industrial Average and invests an equal dollar amount in all ten of these stocks. At the end of the year, the process is repeated. The investor sells the ten stocks and buys the ten new stocks that now make up the highest-yielding stocks in the Dow. Often the same stock or stocks from the previous year will be on the list again. That's OK—you must buy them.

What you cannot do is trade these stocks during the year. If a stock jumps up in price (or down), you don't sell. Trades are done annually only. That's it. As I said, simple but effective.

For 2001, the stocks listed in Figure 17.1 were the Dogs of the Dow.

FIGURE 17.1   Year 2001 Dogs of the Dow

SYMBOL	COMPANY	PRICE	YIELD
MO	PHILLIP MORRIS	$ 44.0000	4.82 %
EK	EASTMAN KODAK	39.3750	4.47
GM	GENERAL MOTORS	50.9375	3.93
DD	DUPONT	48.3125	2.90
CAT	CATERPILLAR	47.3125	2.87
JPM	JP MORGAN	45.4375	2.82
IP	INTERNATIONAL PAPER	40.8125	2.45
SBC	SBC COMMUNICATIONS	47.7500	2.12
XOM	EXXON MOBIL	86.9375	2.02
MMM	MINNESOTA MINING & MANUFACTURING	120.500	1.93

THE BABY DOGS

Reading Stock Prices. Are you used to seeing stock prices quoted in fractions? More and more, they are being reported in decimal values, which will allow you to stop all those calculations in your head!

A few savvy individuals seeking to further improve the Dogs of the Dow theory came up with a twist on this strategy. Start with the ten highest-yielding stocks in the Dow and then select the five cheapest stocks based solely on price per share.

Instead of buying ten stocks, an investor is only purchasing five Dow stocks—the five highest-yielding, lowest-priced stocks. This strategy has also proved effective in beating the Dow Jones Industrial Average.

But Is This a Bear Market Strategy?

In fact, it is. Dividends help stabilize stocks. Stocks that pay dividends tend not to go down as much as stocks that pay no dividend (also note they may not go up as much either). The Dow Jones Industrial Average tends to be less volatile than the market as a whole. If you further buy the cheapest Dow stocks, the argument is that these stocks already had their bear market. If the stocks are cheap, how cheap can they get?

I'm not suggesting these stocks will not drop in a bear market. I'm suggesting that they may not drop as much and may rebound faster as well. As a case in point, 2000 was ugly for the Nasdaq index, the Dow Jones Industrial Average, and Standard & Poor's 500 index. Yet the Dogs of the Dow would have earned 6.4 percent for you in 2000. Not too shabby!

SUMMARY

So is it going to work this year? Who knows? In fact, the more people that catch on to a strategy, the worse it works. The biggest problem I see with the strategy, however, is that you and I are trying to outsmart it.

We will say, "Eastman Kodak is never going to make money for investors. I don't care if it is a Dog of the Dow, I'll just buy the other nine." Maybe you are right, but you just warped the system. I know many people said this about Phillip Morris. You know what happened? They lost a stock that more than doubled from its lows.

Strategies like this cannot be second-guessed. Either you do them as they are or don't do them at all. You don't trade in the middle of the year. You don't morph the system. It always goes back to discipline, doesn't it?

CHAPTER EIGHTEEN

Dividends Matter

"Money may be a curse, but you can always find someone to take that curse off you." —Unknown

As you will learn, sometimes investors make money by not losing money. Even though growth investments traditionally outperform conservative value or growth and income investments, the ups and downs are hard to stomach. As a result, investors usually sell low and buy at the high. The result is that individual investors don't make as much as the growth index.

One strategy that has served me and many other investors well is buying stocks that pay a dividend. A *dividend* is the amount of its profits a company chooses to give to its shareholders. Dividends can be in the form of cash (cash dividend) or more shares of stock (stock dividend). So if a company has annual earnings of $1 per share, it may provide an investor 20¢ per share of the earnings in the form of a cash dividend.

The *yield* is the dividend that the company pays over the most recent 12-month period, expressed as a percent based on the price per share of the stock. For example, if a stock is trading at $10 per share and the dividend equals 20¢ per share, an investor will enjoy a dividend of 2 percent.

Although the dividend may be set for a year (20¢ per share), the yield fluctuates with the price of the stock. For example, if the stock goes down to $8 a share and the company is paying a dividend of 20¢, the dividend yield will now equal 2.5 percent.

WHY DO SOME COMPANIES PAY A DIVIDEND WHILE OTHERS DON'T?

The debate whether companies should pay dividends has been raging for years. Sometimes dividends are in favor, other times they aren't.

The argument against paying a dividend centers around the fact that companies should use any extra profits or earnings to further grow the company. Instead of paying investors, plow the money back into the company, which should grow the company faster and reward shareholders with a higher share price. Any extra cash is best left to management to spend and grow the company.

The other argument against dividends is that a dividend is considered income and an investor must pay income taxes on that dividend. This is in contrast to a lower capital gains tax, which is imposed if the investor simply holds the stock for at least a year. Investors who are averse to taxes are usually antidividends unless the stock is held in a tax-controlled account like an IRA.

The argument for dividends is interesting as well. Proponents of paying dividends say, "Hey, if you have extra profits, pay me some of those now. While I want you (the company) to grow, I don't want to bet 100 percent of my investment return on possible growth." In addition, from watching market action, it seems that stocks that not only pay dividends but steadily increase them enjoy steadier share price appreciation.

▬

RULE When looking for more risk-adverse investments, search for stocks with a history of several years of paying dividends with periodic increases to that dividend.

BE CAREFUL OF A COMPANY THAT PAYS TOO HIGH A DIVIDEND

Two risks that investors should be careful of when investing based on dividends include companies that pay too high a dividend and companies that cut their dividend.

Paying too high a dividend might limit a company's ability to grow. If a company earns $1 per share and pays out 80¢ to investors, not much money is left for expansion of the company. A company that pays too high a percent of its income in the form of dividends would most likely be considered an income investment as it becomes evident that the company's main goal is to provide income to shareholders as opposed to capital gains in share price appreciation.

The company also runs the risk, if earnings slow, of cutting the dividend. If, for example, earnings of the company slow to 80¢ per share, the company cannot give 100 percent to shareholders, which may require the company to cut the dividend. Companies that cut their dividends have not been well received on Wall Street. In fact, there is evidence that stocks that announce dividend cuts initially fall 7 percent or more.

RULE If you are looking for a growth and income investment, find companies that don't pay more than 40 percent of their total earnings per share in dividends.

SUMMARY

A few decades ago, value-based investing was all the rage as opposed to growth investing, which was the rage for most of the 1990s. But now, as the stock market falters and people are searching for a more stable investment approach, finding companies with strong, increasing dividends is once again gaining in popularity. If you can reduce risk and receive income from your investments, why not try? That's what dividends can do for investors.

CHAPTER NINETEEN

Two Awesome Investment Ideas

Over the years, I have found that many strategies exist for finding great investments. Remember that I don't believe in shortcuts, but I've found some easy strategies that have provided me profitable investments.

The following are two of my favorites. Test them; I think you'll agree they are pretty "cool" and easy to implement.

IDEA ONE: BUY STOCKS AFTER ACQUISITIONS ARE ANNOUNCED

It is not uncommon for companies to buy or merge with other companies. In fact, during bear markets, acquisitions and mergers may actually increase as stronger companies buy other companies for a cheaper price when shares of weaker companies are depressed. Usually, the company doing the buying (the acquirer) will pay a premium over the price the stock is currently trading at for the company it's buying (the acquiree). It's wonderful to try to find a buyout candidate, an idea to be explored shortly.

I also believe investing in the acquirer makes sense as well. The stock price of the acquiring company often falls on the initial news that it is buying another company. The price falls for different reasons. Sometimes the earnings of the company is temporarily affected. The cost for the new company may force the acquiring company to reduce its earnings estimates, often causing the stock to be perceived as over-valued, at least temporarily.

Look deeper, however. The acquirer is probably buying the other company to reduce its competition, which may help increase profits. Usually the objective is to increase sales and revenues over the long term.

I searched for a few companies that have made large acquisition announcements and examined their histories. Look at the charts of General Electric and United Technologies, for example, in Figures 19.1

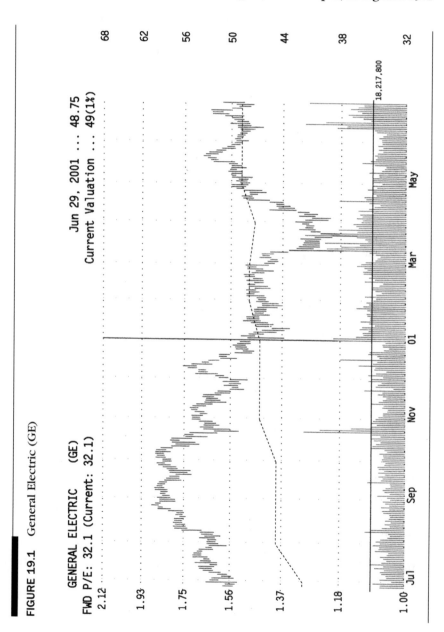

FIGURE 19.1   General Electric (GE)

and 19.2. In March 2001, both stocks dropped noticeably. Why? Simply because they were both trying to buy Honeywell. Even during a fairly ugly market, consider how both stocks trended higher after that initial setback.

In March 2001, Johnson & Johnson bought the well-regarded drug company Alza. Johnson & Johnson's stock initially went down on that news, but the stock smartly rebounded after that. (See Figure 19.3.)

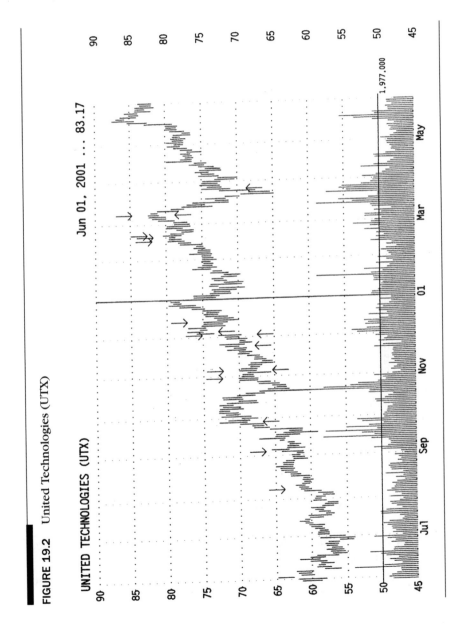

FIGURE 19.2   United Technologies (UTX)

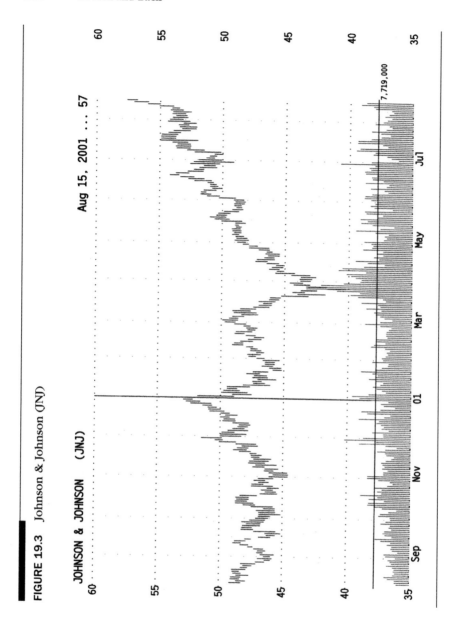

FIGURE 19.3   Johnson & Johnson (JNJ)

So How Do You Implement This Strategy?

- Search news headlines every day (see popular Web sites listed in Chapter 11) for takeover news.
- Log on to the conference call (if available) to see why this acquisition is being made.

- Read the company press release as well as what some analysts think.
- Research the company being acquired. Do you like this company?
- Review the stock of the acquiring company, and make a modest investment in that company if the stock meets your fundamental criteria.

IDEA TWO: DOUBLE OR NOTHING PLAYS

"There's gold in them thar hills!" Through bull and bear markets, but especially bear markets, some stocks become cheap: either a certain sector or, usually as a result of negative news, a specific stock. You may have heard the expression, "Don't throw the baby out with the bath water." This applies to stocks; they sometimes become so cheap that one of three things happens:

- The company will go out of business.
- The company will stage a brilliant recovery.
- The company will be acquired (bought out) by another company.

Buying such a company's stock is a risky strategy because the stock could go to zero—bankrupt. Yet, on the other hand, it's easier for a $2 stock to grow to $4 and double an investor's money than it is for an $80 stock to go to $160. The following are commonsense criteria for assessing a company before committing to a double or nothing play:

- Manageable debt
- Cash in the banks
- A great plan for getting out of trouble
- A solid business model
- The ability by an investor to buy at least five of these at a time (too much risk in just buying one)
- Its stock trading at or less than book value
- Low cash flow and sales ratios

In addition, don't focus on earnings as there probably won't be any. Also ask these questions: Is the company buying back any of its shares? What is the catalyst for making the stock go higher?

Example 1—Individual Situation

Do you remember a company called Xerox? It fell on hard times: its debt became pretty high and it missed a few important earnings

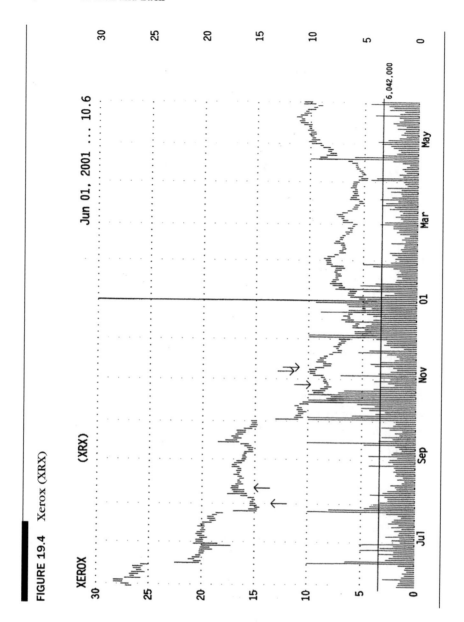

FIGURE 19.4   Xerox (XRX)

growth numbers. The stock dropped from over $60 to below $6 (see Figure 19.4). After a little research, I found this out about Xerox:

- It had roughly $18 billion in sales, yet its market cap was only $6.5 billion.
- Even though sales had slowed, it was still landing huge deals (landed its largest deal in its history with Kinko's).

- Although many companies sold copiers, few actually made them and owned the patents that Xerox did (and still does).
- Banks extended its credit lines (a very positive sign).
- It was trading at close to book value.
- Economic slowdowns can be good for companies like this, as it gives them an opportunity to renegotiate leases and increase sales.
- Many companies would be interested in acquiring Xerox—Hewlett-Packard for one.

What happened to the Internet in 2000 through the middle of 2001? If you said it crashed, you're wrong! It was a trick question. The Internet exploded with more users, more goods sold, and more new Web sites than ever before. Not just more—but *lots* more. It is true that Internet stocks crashed and crashed hard. Stocks trading well into the hundreds dropped to single digits (see Figure 19.5).

Take the case of Inktomi (INKT), which makes Web sites like Yahoo! run. When the stock dropped to $5 a share, it had 127 million shares outstanding ($5 × 127 million = $635 million market cap). Yet INKT had over $300 million in revenue. It was still growing this revenue (not as fast), had zero debt, was trading at a reasonable cash flow multiple and a reasonable debt multiple. More important, although business had slowed, I believed the Internet to be a growth business. The stock most definitely was not worth $168 per share, but I believe it was worth more than $2.40. We bit. As I write this, the stock is at $10.00 After the stock ran up, we were worried about another sell-off. As a result, we placed a stop order on the stock. It was sold soon after. And I'm glad I did. While the stock may rebound, it is simply too hard to assess after the terrorist-invoked economic slowdown.

FIGURE 19.5   Stocks with Dramatic Price Swings

Company	Symbol	Price High	Price Low	Price Aug. '01
INKTOMI	(INKT)	$168.00	$2.40	$ 5.19
AMAZON	(AMZN)	62.00	8.10	9.95
RF MICRO DEVICE	(RFMD)	90.00	8.75	30.00
XEROX	(XRX)	59.00	3.75	8.13

BUY WHEN BLOOD IS IN THE STREETS

■■■
RULE Don't Buy When Everyone Is Telling You How Great the Company Is; Buy When They Talk about All the Problems

A few years ago two very large companies, HFS and CUC International, merged to form one very large company called Cendant. Soon after the merger, investors discovered there were accounting problems; some of the officers of the previous company had "cooked the books." It was a bad situation and the stock dropped like a rock. As I have been preaching, a bad situation often leads to attractive investments.

Although the accounting problems were massive, an investor has to ask, "What am I buying, and is what I am buying worth more than the stock is trading at?" Cendant Corporation (CD) was (is) the parent company of several businesses, including Avis Rent A Car; several time-share companies; several hotel chains, including Ramada Inns and Holiday Inns; and several real estate businesses. CD is the franchiser to Century 21, ERA, and Coldwell Banker.

After the accounting problems surfaced, the stock dropped from over $40 a share to (over the course of the next few years) $8 a share—ouch! The company still owned good franchises, was increasing its sales and profits, and actually was trading at a reasonable value. I simply added up what I thought all the businesses would be worth if the company went bankrupt. Granted, after shareholder lawsuits and attorney fees, the value would be less than the price the stock was trading for. However, I felt that this company had limited downside risk and great upside potential. Either the company was going to go out of business, be purchased by a larger competitor, or regain Wall Street favor and actually begin to rise. See Figure 19.6 for Cendant's climb.

■■■
RULE Find double or nothing plays before the newspapers tell you the stock is back from the grave.

Because the reward outweighed the risks, my group began modestly purchasing Cendant stock, which rose from a low of $8 a share to about $18 a share. As coincidence would have it, while writing this section, the *New York Times* published an article titled "Wall St. Is Pondering Cendant's Fresh Start" on April 22, 2001.

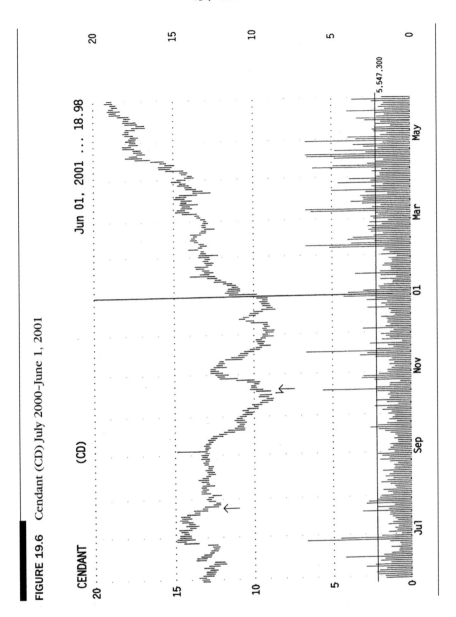

FIGURE 19.6   Cendant (CD) July 2000–June 1, 2001

The article was well researched and insightful, but be careful after reading an article like this. The easy money has already been made. The stock may continue to rise, in part because analysts are beginning to see the virtues of the company. But when investors are looking for double or nothing picks, you want to find them *before* they get analysts' attention. If you wait, chances are you will have missed the easy money.

SUMMARY

With a little common sense and good timing, you can find a nifty investment at a great price. This strategy works well if you are already tracking your dream stocks. When a stock falls into your range, you already have an edge by knowing the company, which gives you the opportunity to buy the stock quickly (because you don't need to re-search it again) and feel comfortable with the buy.

CHAPTER TWENTY

Classic Mistakes of Individual Investors

"Success seems to be largely a matter of hanging on after others have let go." —William Feather

We all make mistakes. Mistakes are very useful tools, as they teach us what not to do again. Me, I'm a recovering perfectionist. I was tired of being disappointed about all the mistakes I made. Now I'm learning to relish the mistakes and review what happened and why it happened.

The funniest part is that we are usually so surprised when something goes wrong. Then, after we review the situation, it becomes clear how apparent the surprise was—a company's slowing sales, a shift in the business cycle, or simply an overvalued market. Enough tell-tale signs exist for us to anticipate much more than we do. Thus, the mistakes begin.

I have made a list of 16 classic investor mistakes.

1. Not listening to what your indicators are telling you
2. Not acting on what your indicators are telling you
3. Not staying true to (or even having) your discipline; continually trying different techniques
4. Taking shortcuts (not doing your homework)
5. Allowing emotions, rather than your strategy, dictate investment actions
6. Selling too early

7. Not averaging more in stocks that have become undervalued
8. Never selling
9. Not properly diversifying
10. Not investing
11. Spending all your money at once
12. Reading and acting on today's data (it's already happened if you are reading it), as opposed to anticipating
13. Following investment fads
14. Not staying informed
15. Not getting rich via your employer
16. Not having focus, persistence, and perseverance

BE CAREFUL WHAT YOU READ

I have discussed how important it is to use your research and not get swayed by the media. Be careful of stories that either pick or pan stocks. Be careful of clever advertisements citing the virtues of an investment.

RULE If you see an advertisement recommending an investment concept, it may be too late.

Over the course of 2000 and 2001, the Federal Reserve lowered interest rates several times. As rates begin to drop, the price of bonds and usually bond mutual funds increase in value. The concept is relatively simple: If you have an existing bond paying, say, 8 percent and rates go down for new bonds to, say, 7 percent, everyone will want your bond paying 8 percent. As a result, you can raise the price of your bond. When interest rates go down, the price of bonds goes up.

By the end of 2001, the Federal Reserve dropped interest rates (the Fed Funds rate) to historically low levels. Adjusting for inflation, the real rate of return on a one-year Treasury bill was less than 1 percent. Without any clever mathematical formula but simply using common sense, I assumed that rates might go down a little more but not much more. In fact, over the course of the next few years, interest rates have a better likelihood of being about where they were in the middle of 2000 or higher.

At about the same time I saw an advertisement touting bonds that looked something like Figure 20.1.

FIGURE 20.1   A Recent Ad

This is another example of investors considering doing the wrong thing at the wrong time: buying high and selling low. The advertisement noted the great return on bonds *last year*. Well, duh! Of course, bonds had a great year last year—interest rates went down. Even though bonds might have another good year, common sense says that unless interest rates continue to drop dramatically, bonds won't repeat the same excellent performance.

Furthermore, I already suggested earlier that after stocks collapse and after interest rates are consecutively lowered, the time is probably right to be looking at stocks again. You want to buy bonds when interest rates are high.

HOW TO STAY INFORMED

The key to finding investment ideas and staying informed is to get out and explore. Here's how.

Create an online portfolio. Online portfolio tracking is a valuable activity. In Chapter 11 I outlined a few of the better Web sites, many of which alert you to news about one of the companies you are tracking.

Keep a ledger. Your ledger is another form of your online portfolio. Expand it to include stocks that you thought you should buy but didn't as well as stocks you sold. You'll begin to see patterns form and will learn from your mistakes. You will get better!

Establish a regular review meeting—with yourself. You don't have to be a trader. Focus on being a good investor. Reviewing your entire portfolio (including your wish list) once each month is more than sufficient—unless an alert appears on one of your holdings or a stock in your watch list.

Request press releases. You are a money manager. Call (or e-mail) companies that you are following. Tell them that you need to be on their press release schedule and need access to their conference calls.

Tap into your network. Talk to everyone you know, and talk to them continually. How is their mood? What are they buying? How's business? This will provide you more indications and clues than you realize.

A WORD ABOUT INVESTMENT FADS

It's so easy to get caught in a fad or a mania. We do it with music, clothing, exercise, diets, and even investing. I live in California, and people drink grass out here! Come on, if that isn't a fad, what is?

When it comes to investment fads, they can greatly affect your pocketbook. The Internet was a recent fad. "The Internet will change the world," the saying went. Maybe, but if the stock isn't worth the price, don't buy it. Automobiles changed the world, too. Unfortunately, more automakers and auto suppliers went out of than stayed in business. The same is probably true for airlines, makers of radios, and producers of every other new and improved invention.

What happens is that a bunch of investors start buying a faddish stock and the stock goes up; those that don't own it become envious and greedy, so they buy in, which propels the stock into the stratosphere. But soon the stock tumbles down to earth. It's hoped these stocks become cheaper, at which point you are allowed to search through the rubble for the best of the bruised and battered. But don't get caught at the peak of a fad.

GETTING RICH VIA YOUR EMPLOYER

I meet and speak to all sorts of people every day. You know who is, by far, the richest group of people I know? Smart company employees. Oh sure, there are a few wildly successful entrepreneurs and a few great investors. Even those that made it the old-fashioned way— inherited it. But the richest people are those who maximize their company benefits.

Maximizing Your 401(k)

We are so eager to invest, but so few of us actually max out our 401(k) plans.

RULE You must maximize your 401(k) before making any outside investments.

Your 401(k) has three things going for it: (1) You receive free money if your employer matches; (2) it is tax deferred; and (3) it's a forced automatic savings plan.

Assume your employer matches 50 percent of the first $3,000 you contribute. That is a 50 percent immediate return on your investment that can't be replicated in a guaranteed format. You must, must, must take free money when it is handed out!

Retirement plans such as 401(k)s reduce the amount of taxes you owe, increasing the return on your investment even further. Assume you make $50,000 and contribute $5,000 to your 401(k). This is an adjustment on your tax return from your gross income ($50,000) to your adjusted gross income ($45,000), which means, you show on your taxes $5,000 less in income. Depending on your bracket, you just earned possibly another 20 percent on your money by not paying taxes on the income.

Finally, any time a forced savings plan exists, sign up. If the money never hits your pocket, you never miss it. Regular autopilot investments are one of the surest ways of getting rich.

▬▬

RULE You are not allowed to borrow from your 401(k).

I could care less what the plan documents say. Your plan may allow you to borrow from your 401(k), but *Ken Stern's School of Common Sense* forbids it. This is retirement money. It's sacred—not to be used for a home, boat, or anything else. Once a person begins borrowing, it's too easy to continue. Then you end up constantly trying to pay yourself back. You may reduce future contributions and, quite frankly, it is simply more debt.

How Should the Funds in the Retirement Plan Be Allocated?

I am a conservative investor by nature. For the most part, however, I believe your retirement plan should be allocated primarily for growth. The fact that this is long-term money and you're making systematic investments at different times during the market reduces much of the risk. Usually, 401(k)s are invested in mutual funds with proven track records, which reduces even a bit more risk.

If you have ten years or more to invest, the plan should be allocated 80 percent toward growth (35 percent toward long-term growth, 25 percent growth and income, 10 percent overseas, and 10 percent aggressive growth). The final 20 percent should be in a mixture of bonds. Notice that there is no cash or money market allocation. If you were not systematically averaging more into these accounts, you should have cash to be able to use when the markets drop. Your systematic investment already has taken care of that problem, so don't let any cash sit idle.

Assuming you will not be using these funds or borrowing from them, and assuming that you will continue adding to the plan, my suggested allocation is acceptable. Understand that it is a fairly aggressive plan that will be volatile and drop during down markets. But it is a prudent growth allocation if you seek maximum appreciation and are willing to accept the risk. Now don't lose your discipline the first time you receive a statement showing you lost money.

What If You Don't Like the Investment Choices?

It always creates a bit more trouble if you don't like the investment choices provided within your corporate retirement plan. You can do one of three things:

1. Find the best choices within the plan and deal with it.
2. Get a group of other workers together and petition to change the plan.
3. Find out if in-service rollovers are an option.

The first two are fairly self-explanatory. The third is not as well known. Many 401(k) plans have a provision that allows you to transfer your 401(k) to a self-directed IRA of your choice. This is true even if you are under 59½ years of age and are still working for the company. If this is an option, I would maximize your 401(k) contributions using the best of whatever the current plan offers. Every year transfer whatever has accumulated to your self-directed IRA.

If corporate stock is an option within your 401(k), limit it to 10 percent of the total value of the investments within the account.

> **I**n the Money. An option trading at a price that would be profitable to the holder.
>
> **Out of the Money.** An option that would not be profitable to the holder.
>
> **At the Money.** An option that is trading at the same price it cost the holder.

Stock Options

Another terrific benefit offered to many employees of publicly traded corporations is their stock option plans. Take advantage of options. Just don't get greedy. When options are in the money, treat them as if they were part of your portfolio. When they represent more than 20 percent of your net worth, sell enough to reduce them to 10 or 15 percent of your net worth. If the stock is too expensive in your opinion (even if it doesn't represent 15 percent of your net worth), sell it.

Stock Purchase Plans

Many companies allow employees to purchase shares in their corporation, a benefit that is usually offered at a discount. For example, if the stock is trading at $50, employees may be able to buy it at a 10 percent discount, which means you are making 10 percent on your money—instantly. That's true so long as the stock doesn't drop below its current value.

Analyze the stock; if it fits your investment criteria, take advantage of this benefit and buy shares. However, follow all the other rules. Sell if it is overvalued or represents 20 percent of your net worth.

Maximizing Employee Benefits

Maximize everything your employer offers: discounts on stocks, 401(k) matching, free stock options. All of these add up to pretty good returns on your investment. As easy and logical as this sounds, the sad truth is that participation in 401(k) plans is still low—too low for the benefits provided.

The one main caution with all of your employer benefits is to not let your employer's stock average more then 15 percent of your total net worth. If it jumps to 20 percent, cut it down. Sell stocks, cash in options, do whatever it takes. If it goes back up (and let's hope it does) to 20 percent, cut it again. Don't let me hear you say, "Well, I know the stock will rise $2 more, I'll sell it then." Oh, no! Not allowed. That is not discipline. You sell when it's 20 percent—regardless of the stock's price.

Remember: *Bulls get rich, bears get rich, pigs get slaughtered.*

SUMMARY

Mistakes are inevitable and, if dealt with properly, ultimately profitable. Study your mistakes. Learn from them. Most important, learn from some of mine so you don't make the same ones.

The Last Ingredient to Greatness

PART FIVE

CHAPTER TWENTY-ONE

My Investment (and Life) Discipline

"Your IQ is not nearly as important as your 'I WILL.'"
—Unknown

The California gold rush is often thought of as a romantic time. The truth is that very few 49ers actually made enough money to support themselves. Ironically, many miners actually found decent claims, but they often abandoned one claim in search of yet another, more promising claim. Rumors abounded and the opportunity for a bigger, better gold deposit was just over yonder.

DISCIPLINE

Do you remember 1999—the good days? The time of easy money, when everyone was buying tech stocks like they were going out of style—even me. Then came the crash. Fortunes were lost. We all prayed to a higher power—if we could just get out of this mess, we would never veer from our investment discipline again.

The economy continued its tailspin. The bear market picked up momentum. By the fourth quarter of 2001, technology stocks had dropped by roughly 70 percent, making it the worst bear market in the history of the Nasdaq stock exchange.

Many of us were caught off guard by this sudden shift in the market and the economy.

RULE When everything changes, we are immediately surprised until we consider how apparent the surprise was.

There were clear signs that the stock market was bottoming. In addition, the Federal Reserve had already aggressively lowered interest rates three times. Yet consumer confidence was still low. We continued to pray.

Then on April 18, 2001, our prayers were answered—the Fed heard them. In a surprise move, the Fed, led by Alan Greenspan, cut interest rates by another one-half percent. Markets began rallying. The same technology stocks that were overvalued the first time were becoming overvalued again. Yet foolish investors still gobbled up shares. Many stocks climbed 30 to 40 percent in a matter of a few weeks. In fact, April 2001 was the best-performing month in the history of the Nasdaq market. Easy money was to be made on Wall Street again. It was as though a sign had been posted saying, "Once Again Open for Business." Even I almost gave in to my urge to buy some of the stocks that were rising fast despite not understanding what justified their price. But, thankfully, I didn't give in to my whim; I stuck to my discipline.

Did I leave some easy money on the table? Probably. Did this mean I didn't buy any technology stocks? Of course not. But I only bought those that I understood and that fit my criteria. Let the others make that seemingly easy money. I was glad for the stocks I purchased before April 18 and for the stocks I selectively purchased after April 18. After the short euphoria of April 18, stocks traded lower for many months.

It's so easy to fall victim to the greed and intoxicating promise of easy money in stocks. That is not discipline, and that is not how to be a successful investor for the long term.

What Is Investment Discipline?

Let's face it: money is a very emotional subject. Not only is it emotional, but because investing is not an exact science, people tend to be influenced by outside sources. To prove this, simply watch the movement of a stock the day a large brokerage firm places a buy recommendation on the stock. Nothing fundamentally changes within the company following the recommendation, yet its stock tends to move higher after the buy suggestion. The moral: Don't allow emotions to dictate how you invest.

A few rules go a long way in this regard:

RULE Forget the high and low for the stock price.

Many investors want to see the 52-week low and high for the stock before investing. What does it matter where the stock has been over the last year? If the stock fits your criteria today, you need to buy it, regardless of whether it is high or low as measured by its 52-week average.

RULE Your discipline is usually right, so don't second-guess it; the best time to make certain investments is usually when it's uncomfortable.

I buy most of the core holdings in a portfolio when it seems that the economy is at its weakest and all of the doom and gloomers think we are headed for a major depression. If you can strongly argue that a company's products and services are necessary and will continue to be necessary 5 and 10 years from now, consider buying the company's stock when it is cheap—when the blood is in the streets and the cannons are roaring!

RULE Never make emotional decisions with your money and investments.

A friend says ABC company is going through the roof. Buying ABC and selling XYZ because you got spooked or because you saw me on a TV show saying I don't like XYZ are emotional decisions that Ken Stern's School of Common Sense forbids you to make.

RULE Ken Stern's School of Common Sense forbids you to invest unless you know what your investment style (discipline) is.

RULE Once you know your style, you cannot deviate. When your indicator gives you a green light, you go.

RULE Make sure your discipline is part of all aspects of your life.

Ken Stern's commonsense investment discipline recommends investors take the following actions:

- At the beginning of every month, update economic indicators to determine your investment cycle.
- Using the top-down approach, determine if your investment portfolio needs to be reallocated based on changing economic conditions.
- At the beginning of every week, search stock screens for new investment ideas. For the majority of your portfolio, search for companies growing their earnings and sales faster than other companies. For the remainder of your portfolio, you should search for stocks that are cheap based on their historic value and possible future value.
- If ideas present themselves, purchase only if your asset allocation model allows.
- Establish an alert system for your "wish list" and "sell list."
- Review all investments once each month.
- Review your autopilot investment program.
- Keep a journal of the stocks you sell.

ACTING ON YOUR STYLE

Economic Indicators

After reading this book, you know I believe the basis for the right investments lies within the business cycle. First, I make sure I am properly allocated for the current cycle; and every month I review the economic screen to be sure I am. If a sector is slowly shifting, I will by and by sell the investments that don't make sense and add to the positions that do.

Weekly Stock Screens

Good investors are a sieve for information, constantly screening for new stock ideas. They get ideas from everywhere—from the mall to where they eat. Great investors thoroughly research their ideas before acting on them. To minimize knee-jerk reactions, I collect all the information in a journal; and once a week I block out time to thoroughly review these ideas.

If I find an idea that makes sense, I find a place within my portfolio where I can purchase it. For example, if I like a health care stock but am fully invested in health care, I have to either sell a less-promising stock or forgo the new idea. But I can't blow my asset allocation and buy more simply because the stock looks good. If I do find a place for it, I slowly begin adding to my portfolio (following the one-third, one-third, one-third rule).

Establish an Alert System

I have two alert systems: One is for my wish list, the other for my sell list. As I previously recommended, we should all establish a wish list of stocks that we want to own at some point. I consider these to be core holdings that you wouldn't plan on buying or selling simply to trade. Decide what price you would be willing to pay for each of these stocks.

Create alerts for when stocks are reaching your entry point. This doesn't mean you automatically buy if they hit the price. First determine why a stock has dropped into your buying range. Did something dramatic happen within the company? Is the reason simply because the economy is changing? Did the company miss an earnings report? I will buy stock if a company misses an earnings report so long as I still believe in the company; in fact, this could provide your entry point.

As I already discussed, it's almost easier to find a good stock to buy than it is to know when to sell. When I buy a stock, I decide on a target price. Every month I review all of my stocks. If one of my holdings had strong sales, earnings, or a reason why I should raise or lower the target price, then I do so at that time.

If a stock reaches the target price, and I truly feel it to be overvalued, I start my system of sell stops, slowly selling and using the one-third, one-third, one-third discipline to sell as well.

Many online personal finance Web sites provide you with an alert system (Yahoo!, Finance, Quicken, SmartMoney, and MSN, as examples).

Review All Holdings Once a Month

I do not look at the price of my stocks every day. Once a week is bad enough but allowable if you don't act on it. Once a month I thoroughly review my entire portfolio. These regular meetings with myself allow me to be less absorbed with the daily gyrations of my stocks. Unless an alert comes up on one of my holdings, I'm not concerned.

Don't misunderstand—I do watch the market every day. If something happens that requires me to act, I'm ready. But usually my alert system lets me know before I find out on my own.

Review Autopilot Program

I will never stop adding to my autopilot program; all I'm allowed to do is increase the allocation. I will, if it is absolutely necessary, reallocate the investments. If I'm convinced the economy will be changing and my allocation is absolutely wrong, or if one of my companies has a significant change pending, I will reallocate. That change could be as basic as not believing in the product to the top manager taking a job elsewhere.

Review Stocks That You Sold

In business, we have meetings after a large event to discuss what went well, and what did not. Do the same for your stocks. Keep a journal of all stocks that are sold. Every month log the new price of that stock. Is it higher or lower than your selling price? What has changed about the economy? If you made a good decision, what was the reason (stock overvalued or economy changed)? If you made a poor decision, why? What factors do you see now that you didn't see before?

YOUR LIFE DISCIPLINE IS JUST AS, OR MORE, IMPORTANT THAN YOUR INVESTING DISCIPLINE

When times are good, it's easy to get soft, but those who achieve the most in life have a discipline. If your mother made you brush your teeth every night before bed, chances are that you still do to this day. That's discipline. Those who have gone through a military boot camp will attest that the discipline, routine, and order learned during this period helped structure their life. I'm sure very few people enjoyed the molding process, but this same discipline is necessary for the investor. It is necessary because a disciplined investor will be less apt to make emotional decisions.

If you allow yourself to go home before your to-do list is completed, discipline is lacking (unless it was an overachiever's wish list). This book would not have been finished if I didn't commit to 400 words a day. On certain days I'm home for dinner and spend time with my family—no matter what. As a money manager, I won't do anything else in the morning until I have reviewed all of the economic indicators and the stock reports for stocks I follow and read applicable commentaries. That is my discipline. If I deviate, I become slack. If I become slack, someone else is going to do a better job for my clients than I do. That is something simply not allowable.

These are what I call *hell or high-water principles,* which means I'm back in Hell if I don't keep this up. If I do, the tide will always be high for me. Let me share with you my hell or high-water discipline tricks.

- Establish daily to-do lists. Every night review that day's list and write tomorrow's.
- Create weekly, monthly, and yearly goals. Stick to them by scheduling all activities necessary to achieve these goals.
- Have an order and a routine. On certain nights, be home for dinner—no matter what is happening. Have a date night (boys/ girls night out). Do 20 push-ups every morning, noon, and before bed. I don't care what your routine is, just do it.
- Be a "Captain" and maintain a healthy state of mind.

SUMMARY

It seems so easy to maintain discipline. But then the newspapers print stories that depress you, or a stock you don't own jumps 50 percent in a day, so again you are tempted to renounce your discipline.

Martial arts contain many different kinds of discipline: Judo is the Japanese self-defense discipline; tae kwon do would be Korean— more aggressive; and tai chi offers more balance and meditation. Although they share some elements, each discipline is distinct. If you were to confront an adversary, you might react differently depending on that adversary, but most would agree that you don't change your discipline. The same is true for investing.

CHAPTER TWENTY-TWO

PMA: Your Secret Weapon

"Attitude is everything." —Saying on a pen from Successories

PMA

You may be asking yourself, How does my attitude have anything to do with investment success? More than you could ever realize. Your happiness, how you look and feel, your confidence, and your frame of mind can make the difference between success and failure.

People with the right attitude are more successful; this is a proven truism. Despite what many people may believe, you don't become successful and then develop the right attitude; this is the antithesis of the truth. I doubt people can be truly successful without a positive mental attitude (PMA). Unfortunately, creating a PMA is easier said than accomplished, especially when times are exceptionally good and we get greedy or when times are exceptionally bad and we get scared.

The other day, while watching a TV show, I saw people searching for rattlesnakes in the dark. And they do this, why? The same people who search for rattlesnakes may think that buying stocks when markets are crashing is ludicrous. Sometimes I think so too. Without the right attitude, I doubt you'll be able to fulfill the task of investing through adversity.

In introducing this book, I shared my story of Hell and back. I had a certain discipline of investing. At close to the market highs, I began to second-guess myself and became frightened of doing (or not doing) the right thing. I abandoned my discipline.

One of the few ways to stick with your discipline is to keep a PMA at all times.

In Chapter 3, I asked what you would do if you had financial freedom. I'll bet your answer included activities not very different from what you do now.

I want you to think very hard about this next question before answering.

"Do you chase the dream or chase the money?"

Explaining this is like explaining the punch line of a joke. Either you get it or you don't. If you chase the money, you will never be happy. If you chase the dream, you will almost always be happy. Understand that happy doesn't mean satisfied or content. I don't want that. Kaizen—I believe in Kaizen!—making the effort for constant improvement. I believe in stimulation, in education. Think about this:

- Those who have no outside interests, such as work, music, travel, and education, have a roughly 50 percent chance of developing a life-threatening disease.
- Those who retire at 65 have a greater than 50 percent chance of entering a nursing home compared with those who retire later or don't retire at all.

Chase the dream! If you don't change your life and do it now—I seriously mean it! If you can't enjoy the journey, you must, must, must change your life.

HOW TO KEEP A PMA

Keeping a PMA is not about abolishing stress. Inevitably, life and investing will be stressful at times. In fact, I believe a little stress is good. It keeps us sharp and on our toes. But do it with PMA. Here are a few tricks to help you do so.

Ken Stern's Commonsense PMA Every Day, Any Day

Constant Reminder

On your bathroom mirror (I assume you look at this every morning), post a note, which is your mission statement. It states what is important to you. I hope your day will be one of education and filled with Kaizen (constant improvement).

Five-Minute Vacation

I need a vacation more than most people, about one per day. You can give yourself a five-minute vacation that will do wonders for your state of mind. Some suggestions:

- Soak a washcloth in very hot water and place it on your face for two to five minutes. While it's on your face, focus only on your breathing. Breathe in through your nose, out through your mouth.
- Take a walk. Always keep gym shoes around, so wherever you are, you can go out and walk. Walk briskly, using your arms and legs. Attempt to get your heart rate up (consult a doctor before vigorous exercise, if necessary).
- If convenient, take a five-minute shower.
- Perform a mental exercise: Lie down or sit in a reclining position; close your eyes and slowly count backward from 30. You may picture going down a set of stairs toward your "happy place." Once you reach zero, visualize your happy place. Make sure you involve all of your senses; for example, if your happy place is lying on a hot sandy beach, then incorporate the smell of the salty air. Feel the heat and the brightness of the sun on your skin. Look at the colors and everything else that is part of your happy place.
- Remember: every challenge in life is a test. Your job is to successfully overcome the next challenge you face.

Play "Number One Concern" Game

The next time something is really bothering you, totally eating you up, take a second to write it down. Tape it to your day planner 30 days from the time you write it down. I'll bet you will laugh that you were bothered by that particular issue!

Work hard, play hard. When you play, only play. When you are with your family, focus on family. When you are working, work. If you try and work a little while playing with your kids, it doesn't work. Whatever you are doing, do it 100 percent.

Diet and exercise. How you look affects your attitude. What you eat affects your mood, attitude, energy level, and how you look.

You probably instinctively know what foods make you jumpy or tired or fat. I love all sorts of carbohydrates (pasta), but they make me look like a pear. So I just don't start. I don't eat that first piece of bread, and I don't start eating the nachos!

"No food tastes as good as looking good feels."

A heavy lunch makes me lethargic. So I don't eat a heavy lunch. I know my eating habits, and you should know yours.

Eating and exercise rules are similar to spending rules.

RULE Allow yourself only one eating vice.

If you love carbohydrates, then have a piece of bread with dinner. But then you can't have dessert. If you want to totally splurge, then give yourself a splurge day once every two weeks to eat whatever you want. I caution you, however, that after you start eating well and looking good, you won't want to splurge.

As for exercise, it's hard to get in there and motivate yourself, but I don't know many people who don't enjoy the feeling it provides when the workout is over. They also enjoy the results it should provide.

RULE Make an appointment to exercise three to four times a week.

Don't break the appointment. You have a better chance of not breaking the appointment if you do it first thing in the morning. If possible, have a workout partner—you can motivate each other.

Have a workout goal: a length of time you'll perform a cardiovascular activity, a certain weight, or a certain pants (or dress) size.

I'm telling you that this will do wonders for you during good and bad times. Once you are in the gym, you must, must, must work through the burn. The following scenario is typical: You get on a piece of equipment. After a minute, you can't believe how hard it is—you'll never make it! After 5 minutes, it isn't so much hard as it is boring. After 10 minutes, something clicks in and you are starting to feel pretty good. Hey, you can lick this. Let's do 25 minutes instead of 20. I feel good. I can't wait to finish and get back (home, office, wherever) and tackle the next project.

After your workout, you feel like a million again: instant stress reliever, instant vacation.

There Is Just Not Enough Time

If you can really get into a child's frame of mind, you'll find that very few things are as enjoyable. If you look at life as a child does, everything changes. A child is discovering things for the first time. It's pure, exciting, and not jaded. When you are involved in an activity, whatever it might be, do it through the eyes of a child—with the same excitement and the same sense of adventure. Eating a new food, traveling, or going to work—it's an adventure. Be curious, ask questions, break down your stuffy walls and have fun. You are taking things much too seriously!

I wake up every day so excited that I fear I might not accomplish everything I want to. I have so many things I want to see. I want to kayak through Mexico. I want to attend a cooking school in Italy. I want to build my company. I want to motivate people and provide more lectures. There is simply so much to see and do in life that I get excited every single day!

Do You Know What's Important?

All my life I have focused on building wealth, and most people would say I have accomplished this. But once you hit a certain goal, including a monetary one, you double it; so while others think I may have achieved a goal of wealth, I'm still building. What's truly interesting is that my most enjoyable moments have cost me virtually nothing.

I have stayed at the finest resorts all over the world. I would never knock this, but my absolute favorite vacation was staying in a little village in Mexico (no phones or TV and sometimes no electricity). I was there to learn Spanish and help improve the local village. Although the trip was very inexpensive, the experience was priceless.

I want to build my company. I want to invest in stocks that go up in value. And yes, I want to make money. But if I make a mistake or life throws me a curve ball, I know that I will always seek constant improvement. I will maintain a positive outlook. I will be happy because of my real treasures: my family, enjoying a fun meal (and cigar) with friends, getting better at a sport or a hobby.

Never Take the Elevator

Perhaps this is a metaphor for life. Elevators are boring and represent a way people can let life pass them by. But when you climb the stairs, everything is different. You worked to get there, so you already have a sense of accomplishment. Your blood is already pumping, and a little adrenaline has probably already been released. This edge will make the difference in your daily life.

Think of everything in your life that is an elevator. Cut them out whenever you can.

SUMMARY

Attitude is everything. Even if you naturally possess a PMA, it will take practice and determination to maintain this attitude during the good times and the bad. Embrace the strategies suggested in this chapter. Incorporate some of your own favorites. Think carefully about this statement: successful people possess a positive mental attitude. If you have a PMA, aren't you already a success?

CHAPTER TWENTY-THREE

You Are the Captain— Start Acting Like One!

"Talent develops in quiet places, character in the full current of human life." —Johann Wolfgang von Goethe

Why is it that two boats can be built virtually identically and contain a crew with similar qualifications, yet, when raced, perform entirely differently? It's the captain that makes the difference. It's the same in companies and the same in life.

To excel in the market, in business, or at home, you must be an effective captain. What does a captain do? Get on deck. Have a clear plan. Communicate that plan. Review strengths and weaknesses. This chapter is a guide for becoming a legendary captain.

What do the world's most admired companies have in common? Visible effective leadership. Following are my rules for becoming an effective captain:

- You must have a focus and clear investing goals.
- You must have a focus and clear goals at work.
- You must have a focus and clear goals at home.
- People need to see you.
- People need to know what is expected of them.
- Stick to your deadlines, threats, and the like.
- Have passion, energy, and the ability to energize others.
- Don't dabble.

Dabblers are just not as successful as Captains. If you start one project today and then go to a different one tomorrow; if you follow one investment discipline today and another tomorrow; if today you are interested in cars and tomorrow stocks—you are just not going to be as successful.

When things started going badly for me in 2000, I clammed up. My group lost some key personnel and started spiraling down. So I retreated further and then I snapped. To hell with being in Hell!

I got back on deck. I immediately created one-year goals. Not dreams—goals. I laid out a plan for what it would take and how I would spend my time to accomplish these goals. I visualized the goals and focused on them every single day.

I reformed my plans. I reformed my life. I told my family and workers what my goals and plans were. I was very clear about what I needed from them and what I expected of myself. People need to know exactly what you expect and don't expect from, and of, them. Even my diet came under scrutiny. I told my wife I needed her support: no more desserts or high-fat dinners. I needed to be in top physical shape to accomplish my other challenges.

When I had, or gave, a deadline, I stuck to it. If a coworker didn't, I told that person that he or she let me down, and then I stopped working with that person.

All of this focus gave me energy. It developed into a passion. This energy and passion are and were contagious. The ability to energize other people is one of the rare skills of a captain.

The first thing I did every morning was to call ten people to network. I looked for new investment ideas and clients all at the same time. I even started kissing my wife again (on the lips!) and telling her how great a partner she is. I held meetings for my team and asked for meetings with management. I wanted to share my vision, talk about what was going on.

SUMMARY

Energize yourself. Have clear, focused goals and plans. Get on deck and make yourself heard. These are the rules of a captain.

CHAPTER TWENTY-FOUR

Summary: The Bottom Line

Investing is a way of life. You will be successful doing things that you love doing, have a passion for, and persist at—through good times and bad. Have a vision and a focus. Don't dabble.

> **"Investing is a way of life. You will be successful doing things that you love doing, have a passion for, and persist at."**

Think about the greatness of Tiger Woods. It's true he has natural ability, but would he be as good without focus and constant practice? He practices, from what I have been told, more than anyone else on the circuit!

RULE Good becomes great through practice, practice, and more practice.

FIND A MENTOR

I have one—several, actually. Mentors can help teach. They are great for bouncing off ideas. True mentors will tell you when you are way off base as well.

HOW YOU THINK IS EVERYTHING

It seems as though many people are envious of happy people, trying to bring them back down to their envious level. Always be positive. Simply think success, not failure.

SIMPLIFY YOUR INVESTMENT APPROACH

This book presented several different techniques for investing: sector rotation, bottom-up stock screening, and asset allocation combine to provide an optimal portfolio.

The key is that whatever you do, K.I.S.S. it. Keep It Simple, Stupid. You don't need to do it *all* to be successful. For example, I talked about bottom-up fundamental investing and noted that fundamental data are easy to find and track. If you just search for companies that have superior earnings and superior revenue, you will probably be rewarded. When the stocks of companies with these earnings and revenue growth peak, rotate your portfolio to the new companies with the fastest-growing earnings and sales. Obviously, this is just one indicator and one type of investing. But if that is all you do and do it with a highly disciplined strategy, this investing style should be rewarded over time.

THE BOTTOM LINE

Hell is a really bad place. Hell is driving home faster on Friday evenings than you do to get to work on Monday. Hell is this sickening feeling that overcomes you when you see your investments cut in half. Hell is not being able to enjoy life because of all your other problems and is no way to go through life.

If you have a personal wealth plan, there is no Hell because you know where you stand at all times. If a little rain falls (and it will), you are prepared.

If you understand the economy, you can profit from its changing cycles. If you have an investment discipline, you won't get so depressed when your portfolio goes up or down. You will either sell when your stocks drop, or you will buy more, depending on what your investment discipline indicates.

Your investment discipline will determine when and how you view your portfolio. You will no longer be glued to a computer monitor watching your stocks. Now you understand how ridiculous and counterproductive that is.

Most important, you know how to stay mentally healthy through your positive mental attitude regardless of how your portfolio is doing on a given day. It is painfully clear how impossible it is to be a success in life and a successful, disciplined investor without the right attitude. The wrong attitude equals Hell. The right attitude equals success. I think you also realize that you may make lots of money. But with a bad attitude and lots of money, you are still in Hell.

SUMMARY

You now have the elixir for everything you need to be a successful investor and be successful in life. Remember Figure 1.3, The Successful Investor flowchart? Go back and look at it; I'll bet you understand it better now. Stay focused on this flowchart; create your personal wealth plan. Based on where you feel the economy is headed, overweight certain sectors, invest without second-guessing, stick to your discipline, optimize your portfolio, and exercise your mind and attitude. That's it. You are there.

It took dipping my toe in Hell to realize it isn't a good life getting sick watching the day-to-day gyrations of the market, not having time for my family, and not having an investment plan. By simply following the commonsense rules presented throughout this book, you already have an advantage. The odds are in your favor.

Enjoy. Enjoy the learning process. Enjoy the education. Enjoy making great investments. Even enjoy the moments when you are wrong and learn from your mistakes.

INDEX

A

Acampora, Ralph, 105
Acquisitions and mergers, 185–89
Advisors, 36–45
    certified public accountants, 41
    financial planners, 37–40
    money managers, 40–41
    stockbrokers, 42–45
    tax advisors, 41
AIMR, 40
Alert system, 209
Alza, 187
American Association of Individual
    Investors, 36, 46
American Demographics, 105
Anheuser-Busch, 94, 95
Annual statements, 106
Art of War (Sun Tzu), 19
Asset allocation, 15, 88, 171–72, 176
    retirement savings and, 200
Assets, 13
    allocation of. *See* Asset allocation
    minimizing nonappreciable, 20
Association for Investment Management
    and Research (AIMR), 40
Attitude, 5
    positive mental attitude, 213–18,
    222, 223
Autopilot investing, 11, 12, 25, 174–75,
    200, 210

B

Barriers to entry, 149
Barron's, 115, 133
*Barron's Dictionary of Finance and
    Investment Terms,* 6

Bear markets, determining end of,
    111–22
    bonds and, 112, 116–17
    consumer confidence, 112, 118
    downside leadership, 112, 115–16
    formal recession, 112, 117–18
    maximum earnings
        disappointments, 112, 117
    monetary policy, 112, 115
    reallocation and, 119–22
    valuations, 112, 118
Beverage stocks, 83
Bloomberg Morning News, 132
Bloomberg Personal Finance, 134
Board of accountancy, 41
Board of directors. *See* Advisors
Bonds, 83, 88, 196
    bear markets and, 112, 116–17
Book value, 146
Bottom-up method, 104, 135–36
Broadcasting stocks, 107–10
Brokers. *See* Stockbrokers/brokerages
Budget(s)
    budget-income ratio, 26
    creating, 27–28
    spending plan and, 27–28
Bureau of Economic Statistics, 70
Business cycle
    contraction, 62–63
    defined, 52–53
    economics and, 53–54
    expansion, 56–59
    indicators of current phase of,
        65–70
    indicators explained, 70–74
    interest rates and, 52–63
    investment sectors and, 77–84
    peak, 59–62